Sea Squirts and Sponges

OF BRITAIN AND IRELAND

Sarah Bowen, Claire Goodwin,
David Kipling and Bernard Picton

WILD
NATURE
PRESS

Seasearch is a volunteer underwater survey project for recreational
divers. The information they gather is used to increase their
knowledge of the marine environment and contribute towards
its conservation. For further information about Seasearch or to
participate in the project visit the website
www.seasearch.org.uk

Published in 2018 by
Wild Nature Press
7 Sandy Court, Ashleigh Way,
Plymouth, PL7 5JX

Revised reprint 2022

press.princeton.edu

Main cover photograph: the sea squirt *Aplidium elegans* and sponge *Amphilectus fucorum*, Plymouth, Devon, by Keith Hiscock.
Spine: *Dendrodoa grossularia* and *Clathrina coriacea*, Anglesey, by Rohan Holt.
Back cover: *Clavelina lepadiformis*, Durham Heritage Coast, by Paula Lightfoot.
Title page: a dense turf of *Stolonica socialis* sea squirts and diverse sponges, Isles of Scilly, Cornwall, by Claire Goodwin.
Contents page: branching sponges and sea squirts, Erme Estuary, Devon, by Mike Markey.

Contents

Acknowledgements   4
Foreword by Tom 'The Blowfish' Hird   5
About the authors   6
Introduction   9
The scope of this guide   9
Squirt or sponge? – some common confusions   10

INTRODUCTION TO SEA SQUIRTS   12
The challenge of sea squirt identification   13
Tunicate evolution   14
Sea squirt internal structure   15
Sea squirt external morphology   17
Feeding   19
Sensory organs and the squirt reflex   20
Reproduction   21
How to use this section – sea squirts   24
Taxonomic list of sea squirt species included in this guide   26

SEA SQUIRT SPECIES ACCOUNTS   29
Sea squirts as nuisance species   43
Sea squirt predators   112

INTRODUCTION TO SPONGES   116
Phylum Porifera   117
Sponge classification   119
Reproduction   120
Feeding   120
Predation   121
Growth   122
Ecological importance   122
Habitat   122
Taxonomy and distribution   124
Terms used in the descriptions   124
Terms used describing surface characteristics   126
How to use this section – sponges   128

SPONGE SPECIES ACCOUNTS   130

Glossary   192
References and websites   194
Seasearch diving and recording   197
Index   198

Acknowledgements

Sea squirts This guide started and finished with two different Seasearch national co-ordinators. Thus, the first thanks must go to Chris Wood, who accepted our tentative proposal on a windy beach in Norfolk and set the wheels in motion, and to Charlotte Bolton as current co-ordinator who then managed it over the finishing line.

In between these points, the production of this guide has been assisted by several fieldwork projects to photograph and identify sea squirts in Britain and Ireland. Liz Morris-Webb, Kate Lock, Chris Wood, Dawn Watson and Rob Spray put together a range of field trips to target sea squirts, together with a group of enthusiastic Seasearch divers. The fieldwork was supported financially by the Systematics Research Fund (jointly administered by the Systematics Association and the Linnean Society of London), Sea-Changers (www.sea-changers.org.uk/seasearch), Porcupine Marine Natural History Society, Natural Resources Wales, and Scottish Natural Heritage.

During manuscript preparation our particular thanks go to John Bishop (Marine Biological Association) for his extensive comments on the sea squirt text, especially the non-natives, and Ian Smith for comments on molluscs. Wilfried and Anne Bay-Nouailhat (www.european-marine-life.org) also provided much guidance and discussions regarding sea squirts, and generously communicated the identity of *Aplidium ocellatum* ahead of publication.

Sponges Distribution information and many of the images in this book were collected during several recent National Museums Northern Ireland Research projects. The *Sponge biodiversity of the United Kingdom* project (2008–11) was funded by the Esmée Fairbairn Foundation, Scottish Natural Heritage and Countryside Council for Wales (now Natural Resources Wales). Additional collections made in the Isles of Scilly were supported by the Isles of Scilly *Marine Biodiversity* project (run by the Isles of Scilly Wildlife Trust and funded by Natural England's Countdown 2010 and The Crown Estate). A series of joint survey projects with Northern Ireland Environment Agency (2007–12) enabled study of the sponges of the Northern Ireland coast. The Sponge Biodiversity of Rathlin Island Project (2006–07) was part funded by European Union strategic funds from the European Union Building Sustainable Prosperity programme. Additional funding for taxonomic work in the Zoological Museum, Amsterdam and Zoological Museum of the University of Copenhagen, received support from the SYNTHESYS Project (www.synthesys.info) which is financed by European Community Research Infrastructure Action under the FP6 *Structuring the European Research Area* programme. We would like to thank all those who formed part of the fieldwork teams for the above projects, with special thanks due to fellow sponge taxonomist Jennifer Jones. Thanks to Julia Nunn and Jennifer Jones for comments on earlier versions of the sponge text.

Thanks once again to Julia Nunn for proof-reading the final version of the entire guide. Last, but not least, we thank Julie Dando at Wild Nature Press for transforming our word documents, photographs and scribbled drawings into the final polished guide.

The authors, publishers and Seasearch would like to thank all the photographers who kindly contributed images to this guide. Photographers are listed on page 2.

Seasearch is a partnership between the Marine Conservation Society (MCS), The Wildlife Trusts, statutory nature conservation bodies and others, co-ordinated nationally by MCS and co-ordinated and delivered locally in England by Wildlife Trust and MCS local co-ordinators. Financial support for the Seasearch programme comes mainly from MCS, Scottish Natural Heritage and Natural Resources Wales. Support has also been received in recent years from Natural England and The Crown Estate.

Foreword

There are many awe-inspiring animals in our world, be they big and bold, or fierce and deadly. Like the celebrities of social media, they are well known, well photographed and garner a lot of attention. But prominence, or notoriety, does not directly correlate with just how truly important you are. Sometimes, you need to look beyond the facade to see a true and otherworldly beauty beneath, and so it is in the realm of sea squirts and sponges.

At first glance, both these animals, for they are indeed animals, may seem small and uninspiring. Certainly the species we see around British and Irish coastlines can often be lost in the tangles of kelp, gloom of the plankton, or clouds of silt from over-zealous fin strokes. Complicate matters by placing these creatures squarely below the water line (save for those hardy few exposed on the low tide) and you have a world unknown to the average human, and often unknown to your average diver. Yet, all these factors cannot deny the true awesomeness of biology and ecology tightly wrapped up by these immobile animals.

Believe it or not, sea squirts are in the same phylum as fish, reptiles and birds and even us humans! It is their larval stage, looking like miniature transparent tadpoles, that reflect their Chordate lineage. When it comes to sponges, these much-maligned mounds of holes and pores are probably best known in your bathroom. Yet without sea squirts and sponges tirelessly filtering the water column, the oceans would quickly unbalance as plankton blooms would choke out the light and gobble nutrients. Sponges are most likely to be the very first life that ever evolved on planet Earth, not to mention estimated to be some of the oldest living creatures, with some believed to be 10,000 years old.

The complexities of their biology, combined with the impact on the marine environment makes the role of filter feeders like sea squirts and sponges vitally important to all ocean creatures. We do not know enough about them, nor understand their distribution as well as we could. Thankfully, their penchant for sticking in one place means they are easy to survey, and that is where you come in! Seasearch is a volunteer diving survey programme that any British and Irish diver can be involved in. By using this book to awaken your senses to sea squirts and sponges, you can report your findings back to Seasearch, increasing our knowledge and understanding of these superbly alien, wonderfully weird and simply enchanting creatures.

Tom 'The Blowfish' Hird
MCS Ocean Ambassador, broadcaster, author and
the world's ONLY Heavy Metal Marine Biologist

About the authors

Sarah Bowen

Sarah took up diving after a try-dive in Connemara introduced her to the underwater world. From there it was a short jump to an impromptu marine life ID session on a liveaboard in the Red Sea, before 'discovering' Seasearch in 2006. An English literature degree and a career in social work probably wasn't the ideal preparation for undertaking a guide to sea squirts, but with David Kipling as husband and buddy, there was to be no escape! Sarah is a keen Seasearch Surveyor, is training to be a Tutor and is a member of Porcupine Council. Particular favourites include hydroids (aka nudibranch food), red seaweeds, and inquisitive seals. With David, she has dived all around Britain and Ireland, including their home patch of Pembrokeshire, islands as diverse as the Scillies, Sark, Fair Isle, St Kilda, and the Isle of Man, and unusual locations like Strangford Lough, Lough Hyne, and the maerl beds of Scotnish Narrows.

Claire Goodwin

Claire first became interested in marine biology after winning a competition to sail on a tall ship at the age of 16. The force eight gales experienced during the trip didn't deter her and she subsequently went on to study Marine Biology at the University of Liverpool, in the hope it would be a good excuse to get some more sea time. Following her PhD at Queen's University Belfast, Claire worked with co-author Bernard Picton at National Museums Northern Ireland where she managed a series of research projects: these included a diving project surveying much of the NI coast, providing information on benthic species and habitats (in partnership with Department of Agriculture, Environment and Rural Affairs Marine Environment Division); and a three year project surveying the sponge fauna of the UK. In her spare time, she ran the Northern Ireland branch of the Seasearch volunteer diver survey project. Claire now lives in Canada where she manages the marine collections and research of the Atlantic Reference Centre – a joint venture between Huntsman Marine Science Centre and the Canadian Department of Fisheries and Oceans. She has dived in areas including the Antarctica, South Georgia and the Falkland Islands to study their sponge fauna and has so far described 73 sponge species new to science.

David Kipling

David trained as a zoologist before embarking on an academic career in biomedical research. He has been an enthusiastic amateur recreational diver, underwater photographer and marine recorder for over twenty years. He is a Trustee of the Marine Conservation Society, a Fellow of the Linnean Society, and serves on the Council of the Systematics Association. He originally decided to concentrate on sea squirts in order to give a focus to his recording and photography, naively thinking that this would be straightforward since there are only a few dozen British and Irish species – how hard could that be? The reality of course is very different, and is the motivation for this current guide to assist in the identification of this under-recorded group of animals. In 2014 he was proud to accept, on behalf of a volunteer project to record sea squirts in Wales, the inaugural Sir David Attenborough Award, awarded jointly by the Systematics Association and the Linnean Society of London.

Bernard Picton

Bernard has been interested in species since his childhood growing up in the countryside on the Chiltern Hills, pursuing butterflies, pond life and birds. He studied Botany at Bristol University and became Diving Officer of Bristol University Sub Aqua Club and has not stopped looking for excuses to spend time underwater since 1970. After a spell at Bristol Museum, Bernard was lucky enough to land a job as a diving marine biologist, working with David Erwin at the Ulster Museum in Belfast. As curator of marine invertebrates with a remit to build voucher collections for Northern Ireland, Bernard taught himself identification of sea squirts, sponges and echinoderms, hydroids and sea anemones. Bernard is author of the first 'Seasearch' guides to Echinoderms and Nudibranchs, published in 1993 and 1994, before the Seasearch project was started. He is now partly retired, with more time for underwater photography and research into his favourite animals, nudibranchs.

CW

A very large specimen of *Axinella dissimilis*. Alderney, Channel Islands.

Introduction

Sea squirts and sponges are two groups (phyla) of marine animals that are often confused by divers and snorkellers, having superficially similar outward appearances. Both groups can be the dominant life forms in many of the habitats around the coasts of Britain and Ireland, given suitable conditions. Our local seas contain over 4% of the world's total number of species of these two groups, yet many sea squirt and sponge species are tricky to identify underwater or from a photograph and are therefore under-recorded in surveys. Records of any of these species will greatly help in understanding the distribution and ecology of these important groups. Additionally, there are some rare species for which Seasearch records would be particularly welcome and these are indicated in the relevant species accounts.

The scope of this guide

The aim of this book is to act as a field guide for divers undertaking *in situ* identification of sea squirts and sponges. Ideally the form, dimensions, surface detail and colour of the live animal should be recorded by a photograph.

For sponges we have only included those species found in Britain and Ireland for which we feel that identification of live specimens in their habitat is possible. It is important to note that many (particularly encrusting) sponge species cannot be identified *in situ*. If in doubt about the identification of a specimen, a sample would need to be taken and the spicule skeleton examined under a microscope. This is beyond the scope of this guide, and we refer the reader to the Marine Conservation Society publication popularly known as Sponge V (Ackers *et al.*, 1992; see references pages 194–195).

Similarly, for sea squirts, there are many that cannot be identified with confidence solely from their external appearance, beyond a general statement such as 'sediment-dwelling molgulid' or 'sand-encrusted polyclinid'. Additionally, the seas around our coast appear to contain a number of species that have yet to be described and given a formal scientific name (such as the 'strawberry' *Aplidium*, page 61). Thus a diver should not assume that everything they may see underwater will be found in this book, or indeed in any scientific literature. The variability in appearance according to specific conditions in which they are found, together with regional geographic variation and changes in appearance during their life cycle causes additional complexities. It is always better to be more cautious with identifications rather than trying a 'best match' to a picture. Laboratory dissection of fixed specimens using internal anatomy would be necessary for some species and, as with the sponges, this is beyond the scope of this guide. Sources of information for anyone interested in this approach can be found in the references (pages 194–195).

The guide is necessarily a 'book of two halves'. The sea squirt section at the front of the book is laid out in conventional taxonomic order and the reader can use the list on pages 26–27 to direct their attention to the appropriate species description(s). Sponges are found in a very wide range of distinct shapes, and although they can be variable within one species, we have chosen to group them by shape as opposed to taxonomy so species that may be taxonomically distinct are grouped together. See pages 128–129 for instructions on how to navigate the sponge section.

Squirt or sponge? – some common confusions

A common source of confusion is between sponges and compound sea squirts. Indeed, the specific name of the sea squirt *Diplosoma spongiforme* (page 45 and image below) recognises its sponge-like appearance. This similarity in appearance reflects both groups of animal being filter feeders. This has led to the evolution of similar engineering solutions, such as large holes for water exit (common cloacal openings for squirts, oscules for sponges), water channels to direct the flow of water, and large numbers of smaller openings over the surface through which water enters the organism. The simplest way to separate the two groups is to remember that a compound sea squirt is composed of numerous individual zooids (i.e. separate animals – see pages 17–18), each of which has its own oral opening. This results in a regular distribution of small, evenly-sized holes (typically circular or star-shaped) across the surface of a sea squirt colony. By contrast, there is very little by way of internal anatomy in a sponge (see section on sponge anatomy on pages 117–118) – it is, quite literally, a sponge – and water enters the organism by way of a meshwork of small, irregular holes in the surface.

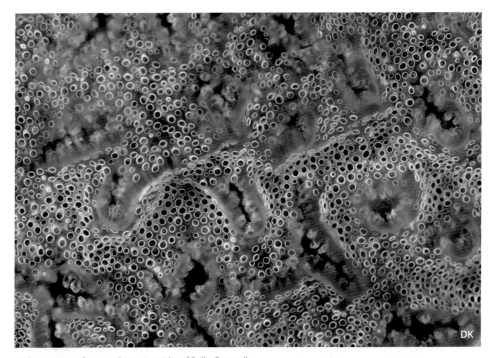

Diplosoma spongiforme, oral openings. Isles of Scilly, Cornwall.

Even with this in mind, there can be some particularly tricky examples. The sponge *Phorbas fictitius* (page 11, top left) has small semi-regular holes (pore sieves) that might be mistaken for sea squirt oral openings, but closer examination shows them to be irregular in shape and size. The *Hymedesmia* species (page 11, top right) has water channels and large holes reminiscent perhaps of a *Diplosoma* or *Trididemnum* sea squirt species, but upon closer examination the surface has an irregular mesh-like structure and lacks the regular openings that one would see for zooids; it is in fact a sponge. If one thinks 'could this have zooids inside it?' then much of the confusion can be resolved.

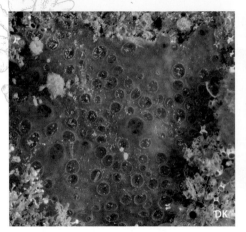

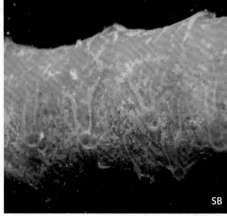

The sponge *Phorbas fictitius*. Pembrokeshire.

The sponge *Hymedesmia* sp. on a kelp stipe. Pembrokeshire.

This is not the only source of potential confusion, however. Unitary sea squirts can easily be confused with bivalves, and it should not be assumed that because something appears to have 'siphons' in a photograph that it is necessarily a sea squirt. Both groups of animals are filter feeders and have similar, fleshy siphons (water enters through one and exits through the other), and thus can be similar in appearance. Indeed, Carl Linnaeus placed sea squirts amongst the molluscs in the earlier editions of his book *Systema Naturae* (first published 1732). The pictures below show the siphons of the boring bivalve, *Hiatella rugosa*, with the rest of the animal (and its shell) being hidden in the rocky reef. Note that the fleshy siphons of *Hiatella* do not have the finely tapered, delicate ends of the siphon of a typical unitary sea squirt.

Hiatella rugosa. Isle of Man.

Hiatella rugosa siphons.

A diverse collection of sea squirts on a kelp holdfast. Pembrokeshire.

The challenge of sea squirt identification

Sea squirts are a difficult group of animals for divers to identify in the field, and this is not helped by a paucity of suitable identification guides. Classically, much species-level identification has been performed based on internal anatomical features. The primary reference materials for sea squirt identification (notably Berrill's Ray Society volume *The Tunicata* and Millar's *British Ascidians Linnean Synopsis*) are 40–60 years old, and focus on internal anatomical features as the key identification characteristics. This requires 'in hand' samples, together with access to suitable equipment and laboratory facilities to fix, dissect and examine the specimen. Berrill's and Millar's descriptions of expanded animals *in situ* are very limited, possibly reflecting the lack of underwater photography at that time and the predominant examination of dredge or intertidal samples, often post-preservation. As an example, Berrill's 1950 description of *Pycnoclavella aurilucens* reads:

> This is a little known species reported from Plymouth [...] It is attached to calcareous algae, and especially to the stems of *Gorgonia* and *Antennularia*.....and is not known from any other region.

As described on pages 30–31 this species is now known to be far more widespread and actually favours a bedrock habitat, such as that in the photograph below. It is unlikely that it would have been found in a dredge sample from such a location.

The white form of *Pycnoclavella aurilucens* in a tide-swept reef habitat. Pembrokeshire.

In the years since Millar and Berrill, scuba diving has become widespread amongst amateur and professional naturalists, and recent years has seen an explosion in the use of digital underwater cameras. A dissection-based approach to identification is unsuitable for recreational divers, who aim to make records based on *in situ* observations or photographs taken during a dive. Fortunately sea squirts are straightforward photographic subjects, being fixed to the substrate and of a size well-suited to the sort of compact camera typically used by many recreational divers. A digital photograph can show a range of anatomical and morphological features (including distinctive colour patterns), many of which can only be seen properly when the animal is alive and actively pumping water. Photography and field observations provide a different route to sea squirt identification than the classical dissection-based approach. This book aims to be a resource for such an approach to sea squirt identification.

Tunicate evolution

The focus of this book is on sea squirts (ascidians), sessile animals named after their ability to squirt water when disturbed. Sea squirts are one of three classes of animals in the Subphylum Tunicata. Their name derives from the tough, unpalatable cellulose tunic that surrounds the animal and protects its delicate internal organs from predators. The other two classes contain free-swimming pelagic animals: the thaliaceans (salps, doliolids, pyrosomes) and the larvaceans.

DK

One of the authors diving with a salp. Raja Ampat, Indonesia.

The evolutionary position of sea squirts has not always been clear. Linnaeus called them 'soft shelled clams', and for many years they were believed to be a form of mollusc. However, in 1866 Kovalevsky (in *Anatomie des Balanoglossus*), noted the similarities between the tadpole-like larvae of sea squirts and those of chordates, in particular the presence of a notochord, thus placing sea squirts in the phylum Chordata.

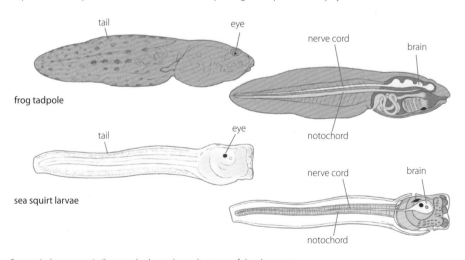

frog tadpole

sea squirt larvae

Sea squirt larvae are similar to tadpoles at the early stages of development.

Within the Chordata, there are three sub-phyla: vertebrates, tunicates and cephalochordates. Until very recently it was widely assumed that the cephalochordates (lancelets such as *Branchiostoma*) were the nearest relatives to the vertebrates. However DNA studies have revealed that tunicates, not cephalochordates, are in fact the closest living relatives to the vertebrates. The current thinking about the evolutionary position of sea squirts is summarised below.

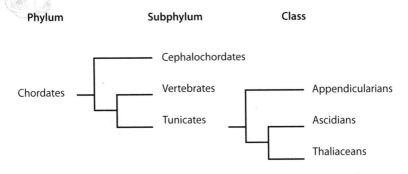

Evolutionary relationships in the phylum Chordata.

Their ability to synthesise cellulose makes tunicates unique within the animal kingdom. This is the result of a horizontal gene transfer event that occurred early in evolution, whereby bacterial genes for cellulose synthesis were transferred to the common ancestor of the tunicates.

Sea squirt internal structure

The aim of this book is to support the identification of species based on features that can be observed *in situ* or in a good-quality photograph. An understanding of the internal anatomy of a typical unitary or compound sea squirt can thus greatly aid the interpretation of a photograph of its external appearance (see section on common confusions, pages 10–11). Whilst the majority of sea squirts have few external clues to the structure of the animal that is present inside the typically opaque tunic, there are some whose internal features are visible through the tunic, and these can assist in the identification process. More broadly, however, an understanding of the anatomy and arrangement of a unitary, compound or stoloniferous sea squirt can greatly assist in deciphering a photograph of the animal taken *in situ*.

Adult sea squirts live firmly attached to the substrate and lead a relatively simple life. They feed by filtering small particles out of the water, reproduce, and take steps to avoid being eaten.

From the outside many sea squirts can appear rather featureless, often with little visible other than the tunic and openings to allow water and food to enter the animal, and waste matter and gametes to exit. Inside, however, are a number of complex organs including its filter feeding apparatus (the branchial sac), a stomach and gut (often with very visible gut contents), a heart, and ovaries and testes. The sea squirt heart is a simple tube that contracts with waves of peristalsis in order to pump; unusually in the animal kingdom it reverses its direction every few seconds.

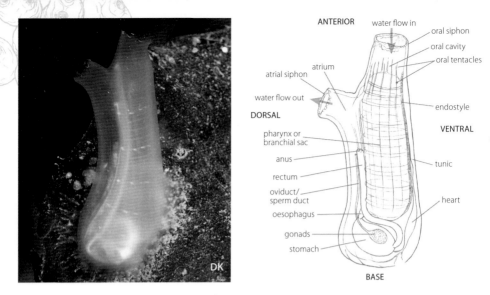

The internal anatomy of a unitary sea squirt (*Ciona intestinalis*).

Although internal organs are most readily visible in large, unitary sea squirts they are also present in the zooids of compound and stoloniferous species, including the minute zooids of compound species such as the didemnids. This photograph of the compound species *Aplidium punctum* summarises many of the features described above. The flower-like overall structure is composed of a series of individual zooids, in which can be seen many of the internal anatomical features.

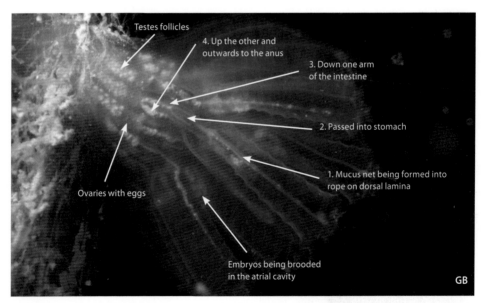

Internal zooid anatomy of *Aplidium punctum*. Jura, Argyll and Bute.

Sea squirt external morphology

Sea squirts are either **unitary** (which reproduce purely by sexual means) or **colonial** (where in addition to sexual reproduction, colonies can grow by budding). Colonial species are further categorised into **stoloniferous** and **compound** forms.

Unitary species such as *Ciona intestinalis* are individual animals that are not connected to each other. They may still occur in dense aggregations as a result of local larval settlement, *Dendrodoa grossularia* (see page 22) being a good example of this. Unitary species include members of the genera *Ciona, Ascidia, Ascidiella, Dendrodoa, Polycarpa, Pyura, Styela,* and *Corella*.

Ascidia mentula in a mixed aggregation with other unitary sea squirts. Loch Fyne, Argyll and Bute.

Stoloniferous species have zooids that are largely separate, but are connected by a basal test and stolon and arise by budding. *Clavelina lepadiformis* is a common example of this form, and likewise the pinhead squirts *Pycnoclavella* spp. Usually the stolon is hidden from view, being covered by sediment and detritus, although it can occasionally be seen in *Perophora* spp. on close inspection (see page 80). However, the inability to see the stolon in the field makes it difficult to use this feature, and the overall appearance of a stoloniferous species (such as *Stolonica socialis*) can be very similar to that of unitary species that forms dense aggregations of unconnected individuals (such as *Dendrodoa grossularia*, page 104).

Aggregations of stoloniferous sea squirts – *Stolonica socialis* and *Clavelina lepadiformis*. Devon.

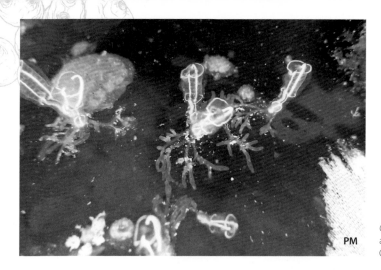

Clavelina lepadiformis on algae showing stolons. Orkney.

PM

Compound species have individual zooids that again arise by budding, but are embedded in a common test and have exhalant siphons that are internal and discharge into a system of water channels leading to common cloacal openings. Examples include members of the *Aplidium*, *Didemnum*, *Botryllus* and *Botrylloides* genera. This arrangement is illustrated by these images of *Aplidium nordmanni* which show zooids that are almost completely embedded in a large common mass of cellulose test, with their oral siphons opening directly into the water column and their atrial siphons draining first into a shared space before exiting through a small number of common cloacal openings.

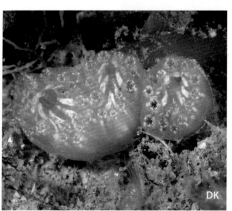

Aplidium nordmanni, white form. Isles of Scilly, Cornwall.

DK

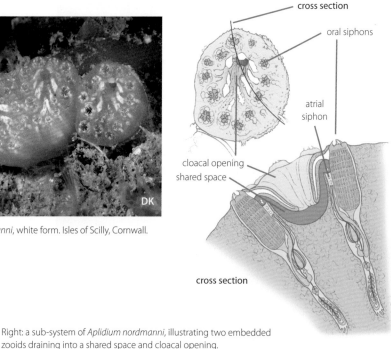

cross section

oral siphons

atrial siphon

cloacal opening

shared space

cross section

Right: a sub-system of *Aplidium nordmanni*, illustrating two embedded zooids draining into a shared space and cloacal opening.

Feeding

Although there are a few carnivorous sea squirts that live in the deep ocean, all species that will be encountered by recreational divers are microphagous filter feeders, consuming small particles of phytoplankton, organic debris and bacteria. Seawater enters by one opening (the oral siphon) and exits the animal via another (the atrial siphon). The atrial siphon opens directly into the surrounding water in unitary and stoloniferous species, but in compound species the atrial siphon on each zooid instead opens into a common cavity shared with other zooids. Water and waste material from multiple zooids then exits the colony via a common cloacal opening. This is particularly visible in didemnids such as *Diplosoma spongiforme*.

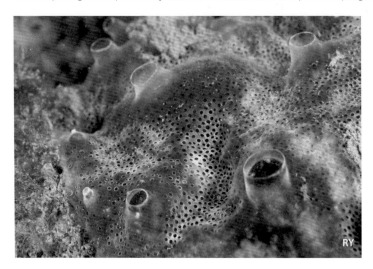

Prominent common cloacal openings in *Diplosoma spongiforme*. Weymouth, Dorset.

As water moves through a sea squirt it passes through small holes in the branchial sac called stigmata, which are lined with tiny beating hairs called cilia that generate the overall current of water through the animal. As a result of this ciliary beating, the flow of water through a large unitary sea squirt can be many litres per hour.

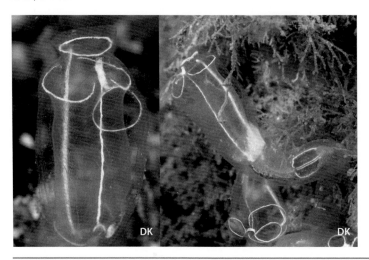

Left: branchial sac in *Clavelina lepadiformis*. Isle of Man.

Right: stomach (red, with white lines) and gut contents of *Clavelina lepadiformis*. Pembrokeshire.

The flow of water causes food particles to be caught in a sticky mucous net. The mucous net is produced continuously from a thin organ called the endostyle that runs down one side of the branchial sac. Once secreted by the endostyle, the mucous net is then moved over the inner surface of the branchial sac by a set of inward-facing cilia. As it passes over the stigmata and into the flow of water it acts as a net to trap small food particles. These food particles, caught in the net, continue across the face of the branchial sac until they reach the far side. At this point the net is wound into a rope by yet more cilia, before being moved down into the stomach and gut for digestion. Faecal pellets are then discharged into the atrial cavity, where they are finally swept out of the animal by the flow of water. In some species the gut contents are readily visible and can help with identification (e.g. *Corella eumyota*, page 77).

Sensory organs and the squirt reflex

Being sessile, sea squirts are unable to swim away from a potential predator. Their main line of defence is the tunic itself, which is tough and unpalatable and can contain chemical defences (such as acid). The weak points of the tunic are the two openings (the siphons), which would provide an easy route for a predator to gain entry into the animal and thus access the soft internal organs. To protect the animal, the siphons can retract and close in response to a change in light, or touch (either direct contact or a sudden change in water movement that might indicate a nearby predator). In order to achieve this, sea squirts have sensory organs that can detect both light and pressure, and are connected via the sea squirt nervous system to a network of muscles that contract the animal and close the siphons when danger is present. These organs can be seen as a series of pigmented dots (usually red or orange in colour, as is common for the eyes of marine animals in poor light conditions) around both the oral and atrial siphons of many species, in particular unitary species such as *Ciona*, *Corella* and *Ascidia*.

Light-sensing oral pigmented organs in *Ciona intestinalis*. Pembrokeshire.

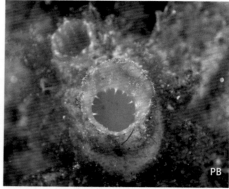

Oral tentacles in *Ascidiella aspersa*. Loch Fyne, Argyll and Bute.

Sea squirts also have a squirting reflex, from which they get their name. This is not the steady flow of water through the animal that is used for filter feeding; that is generated by the beating of cilia lining the stigmata of the branchial sac. Rather, the squirt reflex is a sudden reverse flow of water that acts to protect the animal from damage that would be caused by excessively large particles entering the animal. If a very large particle enters as part of the water current flowing into the oral siphon, it runs the risk of damaging the delicate internal organs of the animal. To avoid this, the oral (but not the atrial) siphon has a number of sensitive oral tentacles just inside, readily visible in many species. In a similar fashion to a Venus Fly Trap, if these oral tentacles physically detect a large particle they then trigger a reflex that squirts water back out of the oral siphon, and so prevents the particle from entering further. The reflex involves the animal contracting its body whilst partially closing the siphons; the atrial siphon closes slightly earlier in some species and is generally smaller, so that the overall contraction of the animal results in the bulk of the water being expelled back out through the oral siphon. A similar defence mechanism for the atrial siphon and cavity is not strictly needed, since the cilia-induced natural flow of water will wash out any large particles that enter, and as a result, there are no oral tentacles on the atrial siphon.

Reproduction

All sea squirts are hermaphrodites, in that each zooid contains both ovaries and testes, and produces both eggs and sperm. These are transported by ovi- and sperm ducts that run parallel to each other and eventually release their contents into the atrial cavity. In some species the sperm duct is readily visible as a white line alongside the gut.

Sea squirts have multiple modes of sexual reproduction, and colonial species can also reproduce asexually. Their mode of reproduction can have a strong influence on where they are found, their local density, and how they move between locations (e.g. as invasive species). A common mode of sexual reproduction, exemplified by *Ciona*, is broadcast reproduction. Here, large numbers of both eggs and sperm are released from the animal into the water column. Fertilisation occurs in the plankton and the embryo develops into a free-swimming larva that eventually settles on the substrate and metamorphoses into the adult body plan. It will remain attached to this point for the rest of its life.

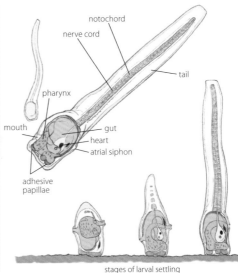

White line of a sperm duct visible in *Corella parallelogramma*. Loch Sunart, Highland.

Post-larval settlement and metamorphosis into the sessile adult sea squirt.

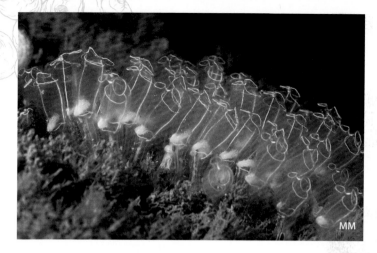

Clavelina lepadiformis with young larvae brooding in the atrial cavity. Isles of Scilly, Cornwall.

A second mode of sexual reproduction, seen in many colonial sea squirts and some unitary species, is brooding. Here sperm are again released into the water column, but the eggs are retained inside the colony or zooid, where they are fertilised and brooded. The sperm from another individual fertilises eggs while they are still within the atrial cavity. The developing embryo is brooded in the atrial cavity until it finally hatches and swims out of the animal. Typically such larvae will settle nearby, soon after release, which can lead to dense aggregations of unitary brooding species such as *Dendrodoa grossularia*.

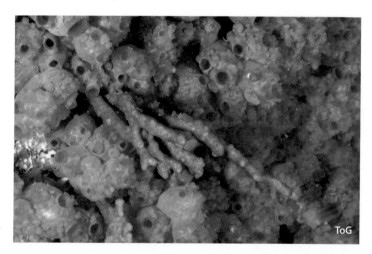

Dendrodoa grossularia with local settlement of juvenile animals. Rathlin Island, Co. Antrim.

One difference between these two modes of reproduction is the size of the eggs (and thus larvae). Because of the high risk of being predated and of not being fertilised in the plankton, a broadcast reproducer such as *Ciona intestinalis* releases a large number of relatively small eggs. By contrast, a brooder will typically produce a smaller number of comparatively large eggs; by retaining them inside the animal this increases the chance of them being fertilised, and protects them from predation. Also, since (almost by definition) the parent will be living in a site that is suitable for sea squirt growth, the larvae of a brooder tend to settle close to the parent and thus do not need to be particularly long-lived. In broadcast reproduction, however, it may be some time before a suitable site is found, and as a result the larvae tend to be longer-lived.

Diazona violacea in winter regressed form. Loch Duich, Highland.

After hatching, larvae will swim for a period of time before choosing a suitable substrate upon which to settle. The exact environmental clues for larval settlement will vary between species, and result in the often characteristic microhabitat preferences of each species. Larvae have sensory organs that can detect both light and their orientation in the water column (up versus down). In some species the strategy is to first swim downwards and away from light, before finally swimming upwards into a dark area. This results in larvae settling on overhangs shaded from the sun, where there is (for example) less competition for space from macroalgae.

In addition to sexual reproduction, colonial species can grow via one of a range of asexual budding processes. For example, individual didemnid zooids can split via a process known as oesophageal-rectal budding to form two daughter zooids. This allows the colony to grow in size without a sexual phase. In other species, the number of zooids can increase as a result of regression and re-growth. For example, the football sea squirt *Diazona violacea* undergoes a very dramatic change in the winter, with individual zooids regressing back to a basal mass. In the following season the zooids re-grow from the stolon and in a greater number than had been present previously, allowing an increase in overall zooid number without a sexual phase.

How to use this section – sea squirts

In the descriptions of individual species in this guide, the general taxonomic classification has been generally followed; there are some species included here that are, as yet, undescribed and therefore do not have standard scientific names. We have given them an English name to aid consistency of recording and ease of updating at such time as those species are formally described.

As methods of identification develop, species names are updated and do not necessarily match those in the MCS/Ulster Museum Species Directory. The names in use in this guide are the accepted versions at the time of publication (summer 2018) according to the World Register of Marine Species (WoRMS).

The species descriptions are in taxonomic order (with the species lacking accepted scientific names placed according to current thinking) as shown on pages 26–27.

SCIENTIFIC NAME, ENGLISH NAME (when used) and CITATION

GENERAL DESCRIPTION

KEY FEATURES
The main identifying features for the species.

SIMILAR TO
Other sea squirts with which the species could be confused and how to distinguish them.

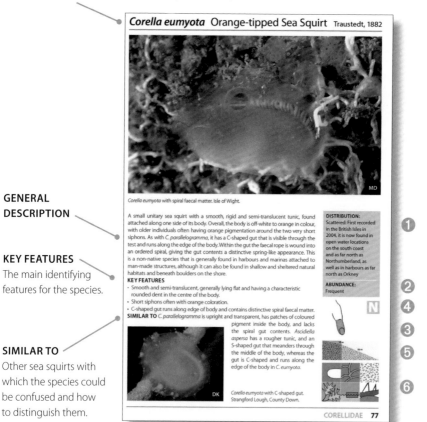

Corella eumyota Orange-tipped Sea Squirt Traustedt, 1882

Corella eumyota with spiral faecal matter. Isle of Wight.

A small unitary sea squirt with a smooth, rigid and semi-translucent tunic, found attached along one side of its body. Overall, the body is off-white to orange in colour, with older individuals often having orange pigmentation around the two very short siphons. As with *C. parallelogramma*, it has a C-shaped gut that is visible through the test and runs along the edge of the body. Within the gut the faecal rope is wound into an ordered spiral, giving the gut contents a distinctive spring-like appearance. This is a non-native species that is generally found in harbours and marinas attached to man-made structures, although it can also be found in shallow and sheltered natural habitats and beneath boulders on the shore.

KEY FEATURES
- Smooth and semi-translucent, generally lying flat and having a characteristic rounded dent in the centre of the body.
- Short siphons often with orange coloration.
- C-shaped gut runs along edge of body and contains distinctive spiral faecal matter.

SIMILAR TO *C. parallelogramma* is upright and transparent, has patches of coloured pigment inside the body, and lacks the spiral gut contents. *Ascidiella aspersa* has a rougher tunic, and an S-shaped gut that meanders through the middle of the body, whereas the gut is C-shaped and runs along the edge of the body in *C. eumyota*.

Corella eumyota with C-shaped gut. Strangford Lough, County Down.

DISTRIBUTION: Scattered: First recorded in the British Isles in 2004, it is now found in open water locations on the south coast and as far north as Northumberland, as well as in harbours as far north as Orkney

ABUNDANCE: Frequent

CORELLIDAE **77**

① **DISTRIBUTION** Some species are very poorly recorded and so the distribution given here, based on existing records, is likely to change as more information becomes known. An absence of records in a particular area or region should NOT be taken to mean that the species does not occur there, just that data is currently lacking and all potential records (with accompanying photographs) are very welcome. The terms used are: **Widespread** throughout the geographical area. **Widespread with a**

bias (normally geographical – e.g. north/south – although in some cases this may reflect survey effort). **Scattered** – a small number of records usually reflecting limited survey effort. **Restricted or localised distribution** – genuine geographical restriction, or because limited survey effort and thus little known.

 ABUNDANCE As with the distribution, the abundance given here is derived from the number of existing records. A species listed here as 'rare' may be genuinely rare or it may be cryptic and under-recorded. The terms used are: **abundant, frequent, occasional** or **rare**.

 SIZE A guide, using parts of the body, to the size of an individual unitary sea squirt, or, in the case of colonial forms, the size of a typical colony.

 thumbnail –
less than 1.5cm

 finger length –
3–11cm

 finger tip to wrist –
15–20cm

to first thumb joint –
1.5–3cm

finger tip to thumb joint –
11–15cm

finger tip to mid forearm –
20–30cm

 CONSERVATION STATUS

N **Non-native**: species which have arrived from elsewhere in the recent past.

DEPTH Shore includes both the lower shore and rockpools and shallow sublittoral habitats down to about 10m depth, **Mid** depth is from 10m to 25m depth and **Deep** is below 25m.

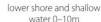

lower shore and shallow
water 0–10m

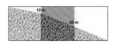

mid depth 10–25m

deep water more
than 25m

HABITAT These icons show the habitat(s) in which species can be found.

 Overhangs Rocky reef inclined beyond the vertical, or with deep fissures or caves, providing a shaded environment.

 Bedrock and boulders Rocky substrate which may be vertically or horizontally-inclined, or broken down into smaller units (boulders larger than head-size).

 Sediment This includes all smaller fractions of stone-derived material (gravel, sand, mud) and biogenic fragments (e.g. shell or maerl).

 On other plants or animals Denotes that the species is usually found attached to specific other animals or on seaweeds.

 Shallow water artificial substrates Man-made habitats, usually pontoons or pilings within marinas or harbours.

 Wreckage Covers all artificial hard substrates (may be wood, metal etc.).

 Above icons highlighted in orange indicate applicable habitats.

Taxonomic list of sea squirt species included in this guide

Phylum	Subphylum	Class
Chordata	Tunicata	Ascidiacea
	Cephalochordata	Appendicularia
	Vertebrata	Thaliacea

Class ASCIDIACEA
Order Aplousobranchia

Family	Genus	Species	Page
Clavelinidae	*Clavelina*	*Clavelina lepadiformis*	page 29
	Pycnoclavella	*Pycnoclavella aurilucens*	pages 30/31
		Pycnoclavella producta	pages 30/32
		Pycnoclavella stolonialis	pages 30/33
Diazonidae	*Diazona*	*Diazona violacea*	page 34
Didemnidae	*Didemnum*	*Didemnum coriaceum*	page 36
		Didemnum maculosum	page 38
		Didemnum maculosum var. *dentata*	page 39
		Didemnum pseudofulgens	page 40
		Didemnum vexillum	page 41
	Diplosoma	*Diplosoma listerianum*	page 44
		Diplosoma spongiforme	page 45
		Diplosoma sp. 1	page 47
	Lissoclinum	*Lissoclinum perforatum*	page 48
		Lissoclinum weigelei	page 49
	Polysyncraton	*Polysyncraton bilobatum*	page 50
		Polysyncraton lacazei	page 51
	Trididemnum	*Trididemnum cereum*	page 52
Holozoidae	*Distaplia*	*Distaplia rosea*	page 53
Polycitoridae	*Archidistoma*	*Archidistoma aggregatum*	page 54
Polyclinidae	*Aplidium*	*Aplidium densum*	page 67
		Aplidium elegans	page 65
		Aplidium cf. *glabrum*	page 55
		Aplidium 'honeycomb'	page 67
		Aplidium nordmanni	page 56
		Aplidium ocellatum	page 57
		Aplidium pallidum	page 58
		Aplidium punctum	page 59
		Aplidium 'strawberry'	page 61
		Aplidium turbinatum	page 66
	Morchellium	*Morchellium argus*	page 62
	Polyclinum	*Polyclinum aurantium*	pages 64/67
	Synoicum	*Synoicum incrustatum*	page 67

Order Phlebobranchia

Family	Genus	Species	Page
Ascidiidae	Ascidia	Ascidia conchilega	page 69
		Ascidia mentula	page 70
		Ascidia virginea	page 72
	Ascidiella	Ascidiella aspersa	page 73
		Ascidiella scabra	page 74
	Phallusia	Phallusia mammillata	page 75
Cionidae	Ciona	Ciona intestinalis	page 76
Corellidae	Corella	Corella eumyota	page 77
		Corella parallelogramma	page 78
Perophoridae	Perophora	Perophora japonica	page 79
		Perophora listeri	page 80

Order Stolidobranchia

Family	Genus	Species	Page
Molgulidae	Eugyra	Eugyra arenosa	page 81
	Molgula	Molgula citrina	page 81
		Molgula complanata	page 84
		Molgula manhattensis	page 81
		Molgula occulta	page 81
		Molgula oculata	page 81
		Molgula socialis	page 81
Pyuridae	Boltenia	Boltenia echinata	page 85
	Bolteniopsis	Bolteniopsis prenanti	page 86
	Microcosmus	Microcosmus claudicans	pages 87/92
	Pyura	Pyura microcosmus	pages 87/88
		Pyura squamulosa	pages 87/90
		Pyura tessellata	pages 87/91
Styelidae	Asterocarpa	Asterocarpa humilis	page 93
	Botrylloides	Botrylloides diegensis	pages 94/97
		Botrylloides leachii	pages 94/95
		Botrylloides leachii var. radiata	page 95
		Botrylloides violaceus	pages 94/96
		Botrylloides sp. X	page 102
	Botryllus	Botryllus schlosseri	page 99
	Dendrodoa	Dendrodoa grossularia	page 104
	Distomus	Distomus variolosus	page 106
	Polycarpa	Polycarpa fibrosa	page 107
		Polycarpa pomaria	page 108
		Polycarpa scuba	page 109
	Stolonica	Stolonica socialis	page 110
	Styela	Styela clava	page 111

The internal structure of the *Clavelina lepadiformis* zooids is clearly visible. Swanage, Dorset.

Clavelina lepadiformis Lightbulb Sea Squirt (Müller, 1776)

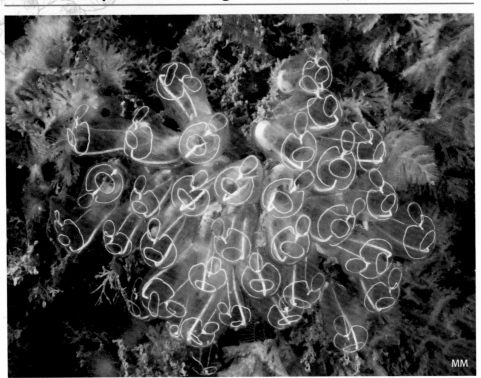

MM

Clavelina lepadiformis. Swanage Bay, Dorset.

This is a common sea squirt in shallow rocky habitats, usually on vertical rock faces and the sides of boulders. Although the individual zooids appear distinct from each other, they are in fact connected by a basal stolon, which is usually hidden from view. Each zooid is transparent, with white or yellow/orange lines, and occasionally a browny-green tinge. Embryos are brooded at the base of the atrial chamber (see page 22), and a small pigmented patch can be seen on the test at certain times of the year marking the area where brooding occurs. Tolerates a wide range of exposure and silt conditions. The Candy Striped Flatworm *Prostheceraeus vittatus* preys on this sea squirt, and the two species will often be seen together.

DISTRIBUTION:
Widespread

ABUNDANCE:
Abundant

Can form large patches in favourable conditions

KEY FEATURES
- Transparent zooids with fine white rings and lines, connected by a basal stolon.
- A small pigmented patch indicates the location where embryos are brooded.
- Can form extensive colonies.

SIMILAR TO *Diazona violacea* has similar but not identical markings, a test that is more opaque and milky, and zooids united in a common test rather than as individuals connected by creeping stolons.

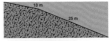

Pycnoclavella spp. Pinhead sea squirts

The golden form of *Pycnoclavella aurilucens* covering an extensive area of reef. Pembrokeshire.

Three species of *Pycnoclavella* are found in British and Irish waters: *P. aurilicens*, *P. producta*, and *P. stolonialis*. The individual species can be differentiated by their coloration and, in the case of *P. producta*, by their relative size. All are stoloniferous, with individual transparent pinhead-sized zooids connected by a creeping stolon that is hidden from view. Typically found attached to rock in areas with high levels of water movement, *P. aurilucens* in particular can form extensive colonies over hard substrates, often interspersed with *P. stolonialis* and *P. producta*.

KEY FEATURES

- Extremely small transparent zooids that can form extensive colonies.
- *P. aurilucens* has three golden or white spots around the siphons.
- *P. producta* is slightly larger and has no pigmented markings.
- *P. stolonialis* is identical in size with a white (or occasionally beige) saddle between the two siphon openings in the shape of a Maltese Cross.

SIMILAR TO *Clavelina lepadiformis* has a similar body shape, but is much bigger and with different coloration. *Pycnoclavella* species can be readily distinguished from other small transparent stoloniferous species, such as *Perophora*, by their markings and body shape.

DISTRIBUTION *P. aurilucens* is mainly a south-western species, with the majority of records from south-west England and Wales, although there are isolated records from Northern Ireland, the west of Scotland and north Norfolk. *P. producta* is mainly found along the south coast, Pembrokeshire and north Norfolk. *P. stolonialis* is predominantly a south-west and Irish Sea species.

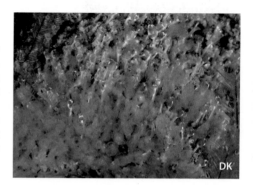

Mixed aggregation of *Pycnoclavella producta* and both colour forms of *P. aurilucens*. Pembrokeshire.

Pycnoclavella aurilucens

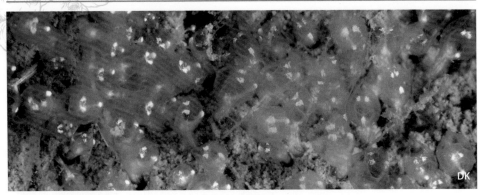

Both white and golden forms of *Pycnoclavella aurilucens* with the characteristic three dots on each zooid. Pembrokeshire.

Heavily pigmented individuals of *Pycnoclavella aurilucens* on a rocky reef. Pembrokeshire.

DISTRIBUTION:
Widespread with a bias / scattered

ABUNDANCE:
Frequent

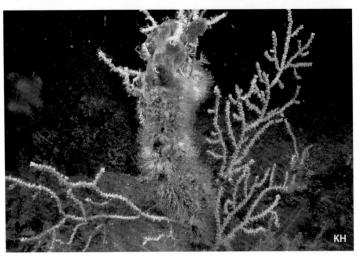

As originally described, *Pycnoclavella aurilucens* is often found growing on the Pink Sea Fan, *Eunicella verrucosa*. Devon.

Pycnoclavella producta (Milne Edwards, 1841)

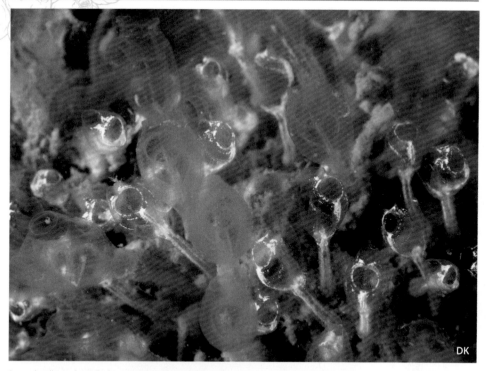

Pycnoclavella producta (lacking pigmentation) with smaller white *P. aurilucens*. Pembrokeshire.

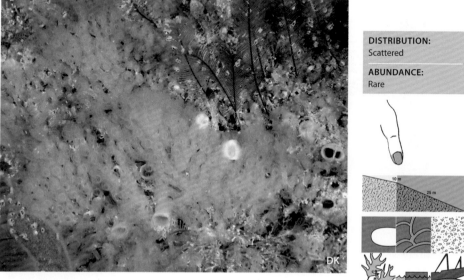

Pycnoclavella producta with white siphons of *Polycarpa scuba*. Pembrokeshire.

DISTRIBUTION:
Scattered

ABUNDANCE:
Rare

White 'Maltese Cross' pigmentation between the siphons of *Pycnoclavella stolonialis*. Pembrokeshire.

DISTRIBUTION:
Scattered: not in Scotland

ABUNDANCE:
Occasional

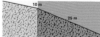

Colonies of *Pycnoclavella stolonialis* tend to be smaller, with zooids more widely spaced. Pembrokeshire.

JL

Diazona violacea. Sound of Mull.

A very distinctive species that can form large ball-shaped colonies from which multiple white-marked translucent zooids emerge. In winter the zooids of *Diazona* regress to leave an overwintering milky jelly-like mass. Favours rock ledges or stable boulders, most often at depths of over 20m.

KEY FEATURES

- Large globular colonies formed of translucent zooids originating from a common base.
- White markings on individual zooids, including six small spots around the atrial siphon.

A partially regressed colony of *Diazona violacea*. Isles of Scilly, Cornwall.

SB

DISTRIBUTION:
Widespread with a bias: mostly the west coasts of Britain and Ireland, particularly Scotland and the south coast.

ABUNDANCE:
Frequent

Colonies can grow to more than head-sized

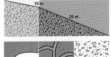

Different sized colonies on *Diazona violacea* on a vertical reef face. Plymouth, Devon.

SIMILAR TO A full-sized colony is unlikely to be mistaken for any other British species. *Clavelina lepadiformis* has transparent and less swollen zooids, and a different arrangement of white pigmentation. Occasionally, small specimens of *Diazona* consisting of only a few individual zooids can be found, and care should be taken to look at the overall milkiness and pattern of markings when making an identification.

Right: a small colony of *Diazona violacea* showing the individual zooid markings. Firth of Lorn, Argyll and Bute.

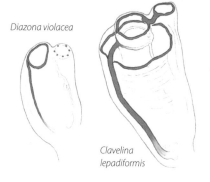

Diazona violacea

Clavelina lepadiformis

A young zooid of *Diazona violacea* (white, centre) surrounded by *Clavelina lepadiformis*. Sound of Mull.

Highlighted areas illustrate the different zooid pigmentation in these two species.

Didemnum coriaceum
(Drasche, 1883)

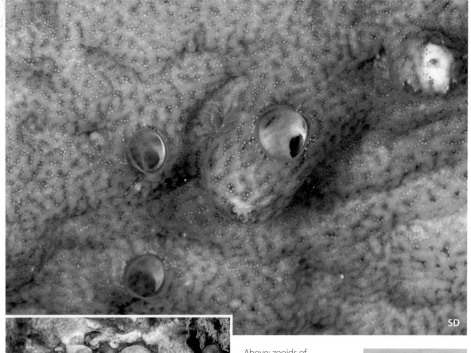

SD

RY

Above: zooids of *Didemnum coriaceum* are restricted to the dark pigmented areas. Sark, Channel Islands.

Left: three-dimensional and shiny appearance of *Didemnum coriaceum*. Devon.

DISTRIBUTION:
Scattered: a southern species currently restricted to Cornwall, Pembrokeshire and parts of the south coast of England across to the Channel Islands.

ABUNDANCE:
Rare

A spiculose didemnid with a shiny surface that has the consistency of leather. It has a variable, two-tone coloration formed of an overall white, grey or purple base broken up with darker markings of yellow, orange or brown. The zooids appear grouped into loosely organized clusters, forming lines that are largely restricted to the darker areas, with the lighter zones being generally zooid-free. It favours areas with strong water movement where it can be abundant on algal holdfasts, hard substrates, and growing over the shells of animals such as mussels.

KEY FEATURES
- Two-tone in colour with a shiny, clean appearance.
- Zooids clustered into lines that have a darker pigmentation, separated by lighter-coloured zooid-free areas.

SIMILAR TO Can be difficult to distinguish from large sheets of two-tone *D. maculosum* (see opposite and page 38), although the latter can often appear hairy and has zooids more evenly distributed over both light and dark areas.

Above: *Didemnum coriaceum* overgrowing mussels in a tide-swept habitat. Pembrokeshire.

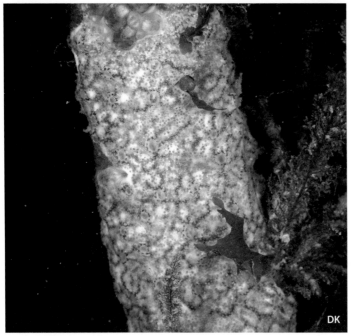

Didemnum maculosum showing zooids present in both light and dark areas. Pembrokeshire.

Didemnum maculosum (Milne Edwards, 1841)

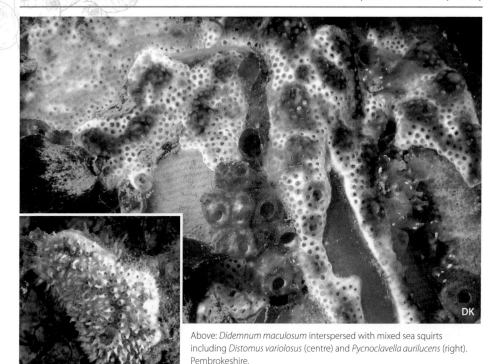

Above: *Didemnum maculosum* interspersed with mixed sea squirts including *Distomus variolosus* (centre) and *Pycnoclavella aurilucens* (right). Pembrokeshire.

Left: *Didemnum maculosum* with projections from each zooid giving a 'hairy' appearance. Llŷn Peninsula, Gwynedd.

A spiculose didemnid with a two-tone coloration, usually white with grey and purple blotches. It has a mottled appearance with small, regular inhalant pores and larger, fairly inconspicuous cloacal openings, and can often appear hairy. It is most often found growing on, or at the bases of, kelp stipes.

There is a variety termed *D. maculosum* var. *dentata* (see opposite) that shows identical internal zooid morphology and cannot be separated from *D. maculosum*. This 'snowflake' variant is found only in pure white, and forms numerous small colonies scattered over the substrate. Each zooid has a three-pointed projection, giving the colony a spiky appearance.

For recording purposes, both forms should be noted separately.

KEY FEATURES
- The classic variety has a two-tone coloration and can form large sheets, with a surface that can be hairy in appearance.
- *D. maculosum* var. *dentata* forms small pure white scattered patches with a spiky appearance.

SIMILAR TO *D. coriaceum* is very similar to the two-tone variant of *D. maculosum*, but the former has a much more obvious multi-coloured appearance and does not have the hairy appearance of *D. maculosum*. Furthermore, in *D. coriaceum* the zooids are largely restricted to the darker areas. *D. maculosum* var. *dentata* could be mistaken for *Lissoclinum perforatum*, which is also pure white in colour. However, *L. perforatum* has a smooth colony margin, a noticeable 'perforated' appearance and is generally found in single larger patches.

DISTRIBUTION:
Widespread

ABUNDANCE:
Frequent

var. *dentata*

Didemnum maculosum var. dentata

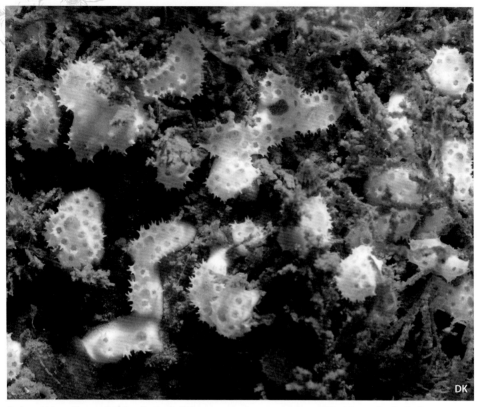

DK

Each zooid has a three-pointed projection in *Didemnum maculosum* var. *dentata*. Milford Haven, Pembrokeshire.

KH

'Snowflake' scattering of colonies of *Didemnum maculosum* var. *dentata* over a reef. Plymouth, Devon.

Didemnum pseudofulgens Médioni, 1970

Didemnum pseudofulgens showing less-pigmented areas extending from the cloacal openings. Pembrokeshire.

A spiculose didemnid that forms small, orange-red irregular patches. The inhalant pores are regularly spaced except for semi-transparent zooid- and pigment-free areas leading from the cloacal openings, which resemble dribbles of paint. In the right geographical location, it seems to tolerate a wide range of habitats, from current-swept pinnacles to sheltered bays. It is typically found on vertical rock faces with some silt.

KEY FEATURES
- Deep orange colour.
- A shiny appearance and diagnostic less-pigmented areas extending from the cloacal openings.

SIMILAR TO This is a distinctive sea squirt which once seen is unlikely to be confused with any other didemnid owing to its colour and areas empty of both zooids and pigmentation.

DISTRIBUTION:
Scattered: currently known from Pembrokeshire, North Wales, Strangford Lough, Cornwall and Dorset.

ABUNDANCE:
Rare

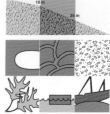

Didemnum pseudofulgens on a vertical reef face. Pembrokeshire.

Didemnum vexillum Carpet Sea Squirt Kott, 2002

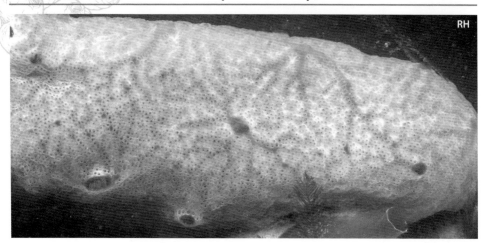

Underwater close-up with zooids and cloacal openings open. Holyhead Marina, Anglesey.

A spiculose didemnid forming colonies of a single colour (off-white, cream or dull orange) lacking black or brown markings. Colonies are relatively thin (2–5mm) and flexible, but quite tough – often almost leathery – and can generally be peeled off the substrate in large pieces. Colonies can become large in size, and when on vertical or overhanging surfaces sometimes produce long dangling lobes that can detach and fall away as viable fragments.

Overall, colonies have a lightly veined and mottled appearance produced by a combination of pale areas of dense spicules and darker water channels. The channels are particularly noticeable in the vicinity of the cloacal openings. Inhalant openings are numerous and unmarked, and the occasional larger cloacal openings are similarly unmarked.

Out of the water (or when otherwise disturbed), each tightly contracted inhalant opening is marked by a white spot where the surrounding spicules have been piled together. The darker water channels are usually still visible in places.

DISTRIBUTION:
Scattered: has occurred primarily as fouling species in marinas and aquaculture sites (S England, N Wales, W Scotland, Strangford Lough), but also North Sea wrecks and recently spreading onto shore and mixed seabed (N Kent) and likely to become more widespread.

ABUNDANCE:
Occasional (but locally abundant)

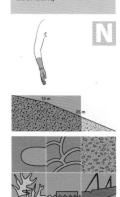

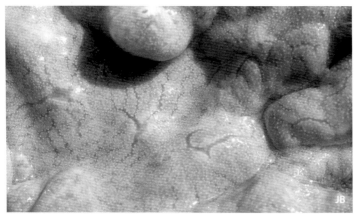

Out of water, everything closed up; white spots indicate zooids.

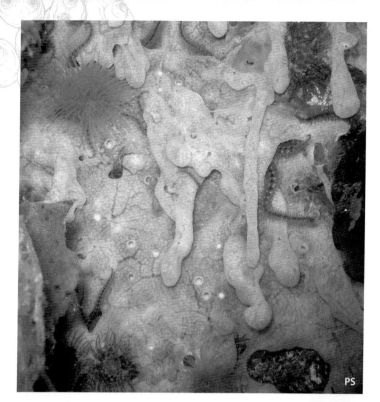

Underwater view of a larger colony. Firth of Clyde.

PS

IMPORTANT NOTE *D. vexillum* is a non-native species that is a nuisance in many areas of the world, where it can have significant negative impacts on both benthic habitats (e.g. Georges Bank, Massachusetts) and aquaculture (see image right). In Britain and Ireland it is a priority invasive species, and potential sightings (including a photograph) should be reported to www.brc.ac.uk/risc/alert.php?species=carpet_seasquirt

KEY FEATURES
- Single-colour colonies
- Darker-toned water channels
- Complete absence of any dark pigmentation
- Colonies relatively tough and peelable
- Each zooid marked by a white spot when contracted.

SIMILAR TO *D. vexillum* is similar to several other didemnid species and is relatively lacking in clear-cut features. Consistency, visible water channels, and absence of blackish pigmentation (either in patches or as fine circles around the colony openings) distinguish it from many commonly encountered *Didemnum* and *Trididemnum* species. *Trididemnum cereum* in particular can form similar lobulose, three-dimensional colonies. *Diplosoma* sp. 1 can also grow large and achieve very high coverage, but is extremely soft, flimsy and easily torn. Some sponges have also been mistaken for *D. vexillum*. Given the similarity to other species and its importance as a nuisance non-native, potential sightings of *D. vexillum* should be verified via the link above before inclusion on Seasearch forms.

Showing *D. vexillum* acting as a nuisance species, encrusting mussel cages.

USGS

Sea squirts as nuisance species

Sea squirts have a significant global economic impact as invasive and biofouling organisms. Recent years have seen the arrival in Britain and Ireland of the non-native species *Didemnum vexillum*, *Corella eumyota*, *Perophora japonica*, *Asterocarpa humilis*, *Botrylloides violaceus* and *B. diegensis*. Sea squirts readily spread globally; the occurrence of *Styela clava* in British and Irish waters is believed to have been the result of ships returning to Plymouth from the Korean War. With ever-increasing levels of global shipping, nuisance non-native sea squirts pose a significant potential threat to marine habitats and biodiversity due to their rapid proliferation and ability to filter planktonic organisms out of the food chain.

The Carpet Sea Squirt *Didemnum vexillum* (page 41) is a species of particular global concern. It has almost entirely smothered the benthic substrate of many tens of square miles of the important fishery grounds at Georges Bank off Massachusetts. The ability of *D. vexillum* to grow by asexual methods allows the easy spread of colony fragments. This has been suggested to have led to its increased spread in Georges Bank as a result of the use of bottom-towed gear breaking up colonies, and fragments then settling further downstream to start new colonies. The discovery of *D. vexillum* in Holyhead Marina led to eradication measures being taken over concerns regarding the potential impact on nearby shellfish aquaculture.

Ciona intestinalis covering the SS *Port Napier*, Isle of Skye, Highland.

Marinas are the most common locations for non-native species to gain a foothold. A number of species can be present in high numbers in marina environments, where the restricted water exchange can facilitate reproduction and floating man-made structures provide an unusual shallow water substrate that does not dry out. Boat traffic also provides a ready mechanism to transfer attached individuals between marinas. The weight of attached organisms on ropes and other artificial structures can make sea squirts nuisance biofoulers, as shown here.

Some native British and Irish species are a nuisance elsewhere in the world. *Ciona intestinalis* is native to Britain and Ireland

One of the authors inspecting a rope fouled predominantly with *Ascidiella aspersa* in a Suffolk marina.

and not viewed as a nuisance species, perhaps except in the specialised environment of a marina, and can form dense aggregations on both natural and artificial structures. Interestingly, the mussel fishery in Prince Edward Island (Canada) has been severely impacted by the spread of *C. intestinalis* (non-native to that particular area), which find mussel ropes excellent substrates upon which to grow. Current mitigation measures include fitting high-pressure water sprays to boats harvesting the mussels, which selectively remove the soft *Ciona* while leaving the hard-shelled bivalves intact.

Diplosoma listerianum
(Milne Edwards, 1841)

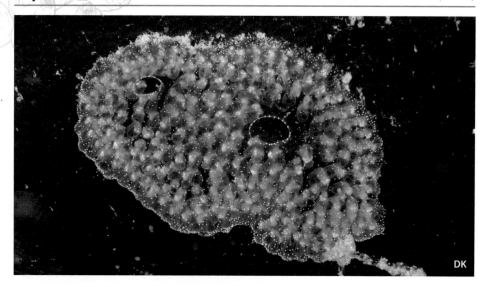

DK

A non-spiculose didemnid that is soft and fragile to the touch. Colonies are transparent and gelatinous, with a pattern of small yellow/white pigment bodies in the surface layer. The zooids are scattered densely throughout the sheet, and are visible through the transparent test, interspersed with occasional larger cloacal openings that are not conspicuously pigmented. Unusually for a didemnid, the inhalant pores are simple circles, as opposed to the more star-like openings in the spiculose didemnids. This is a common sea squirt in shallow water, typically found in patches on algae.

Speckled pigmentation in a small colony of *Diplosoma listerianum* on algae. Isle of Skye, Highland.

KEY FEATURES
- Transparent gelatinous colonies with speckles of pigmentation.
- Typically found as small colonies in shallow water on algae.

SIMILAR TO *Diplosoma spongiforme* forms larger, more heavily pigmented sheets on hard substrates, typically in deeper water with more current action, whereas *D. listerianum* is found shallower, in smaller patches, and on algae. Another *Diplosoma* species is found in several semi-enclosed habitats and is characterised by forming large sheets, often over the surface of other sessile life (see *Diplosoma* sp. 1, page 47).

DISTRIBUTION:
Widespread

ABUNDANCE:
Frequent

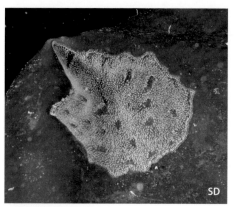

SD

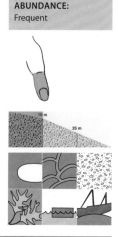

Diplosoma listerianum with multiple cloacal openings, on algae. Sark, Channel Islands.

Diplosoma spongiforme (Giard, 1872)

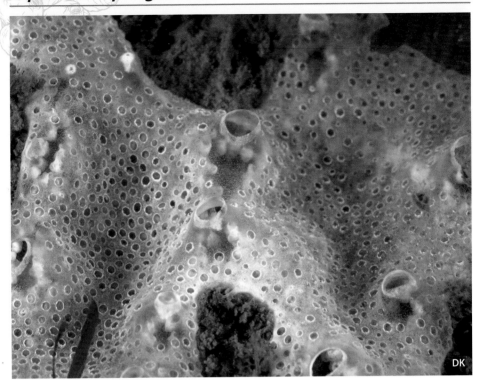

The prominent cloacal openings of *Diplosoma spongiforme* resemble sponge oscules. Pembrokeshire.

A non-spiculose didemnid that is very delicate to the touch. Forms extensive transparent sheets covering rocks and other hard surfaces, often on corners, or rock exposed to water movement. The zooids are small and pigmented, and are scattered throughout the sheet. Largely transparent but variable in coloration, often with a bluish-white or greenish tinge. Unusually for a didemnid, the inhalant pores are simple white-rimmed circles, as opposed to the more star-like openings in the spiculose didemnids. Cloacal openings are large and conspicuous with white rims

DISTRIBUTION:
Widespread

ABUNDANCE:
Frequent

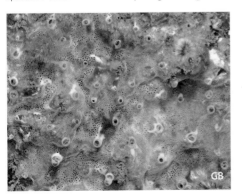

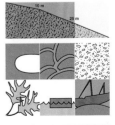

Diplosoma spongiforme with heavily pigmented cloacal openings. Sark, Channel Islands.

Diplosoma spongiforme is often found on the corners of rock and wrecks. Lyme Bay, Devon/Dorset.

that often form oscule-like chimneys, giving this species a characteristic sponge-like appearance from which it derives its name. Common in a wide variety of habitats, ranging from sheltered to exposed conditions.

KEY FEATURES
- Transparent and delicate colonies that form extensive sheets on hard substrates.
- Circular white-rimmed inhalant openings.
- White markings around prominent raised cloacal openings

SIMILAR TO *Diplosoma listerianum* is typically found in much smaller patches, on algae, and lacks the large white-rimmed cloacal openings.

Diplosoma spongiforme is very variable in its pigmentation. Weymouth Bay, Dorset.

Diplosoma sp. 1

Diplosoma sp. 1 growing over cobbles and pebbles. Milford Haven, Pembrokeshire.

A non-spiculose didemnid that is soft and fragile to the touch. It forms very extensive sheets, typically growing over other sessile life. Abundant in shallow water semi-enclosed habitats such as marinas and harbours where invasive non-native species are present.

KEY FEATURES
- A vigorously growing *Diplosoma* species, often found overgrowing other sessile life.
- No pigment bodies in the surface layer of the sheet.

SIMILAR TO The relationship of this species to *D. listerianum* is unclear; it is being treated separately as it lacks the white pigment speckles of *D. listerianum* and has a much more vigorous growth habit. *D. spongiforme* is more pigmented and found in open reef habitats.

DISTRIBUTION:
Restricted or localised distribution: known from Milford Haven, Portland Marina, Blackwater Estuary, Loch Creran, Strangford Lough

ABUNDANCE:
Rare: as so little known

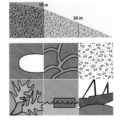

Diplosoma sp. 1 growing over a serpulid worm reef. Loch Creran, Argyll and Bute.

Lissoclinum perforatum (Giard, 1872)

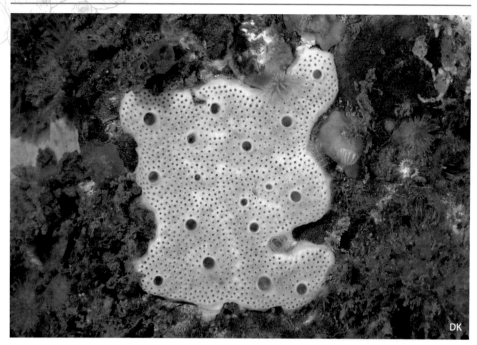

A larger colony of *Lissoclinum perforatum* with its characteristic perforated appearance. Farne Islands, Northumberland.

A spiculose didemnid that forms compact, pure white colonies on hard substrates. The colony edges are rounded and the surface smooth. The inhalant pores are scattered regularly over the surface, and the cloacal openings have a raised rim. The pores are clean-edged and circular, giving the appearance of having been punched into the surface (hence *perforatum*). It is found in exposed sites and places with strong tidal streams.

KEY FEATURES
- Neat, pure white colonies.
- Smooth-edged holes give a distinctive perforated appearance.

SIMILAR TO *L. weigelei* has distinctive brown markings. Most other spiculose didemnids have at least two colours and inhalant pores that are generally more star-like.

DISTRIBUTION:
Widespread

ABUNDANCE:
Abundant

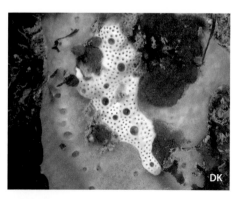

A typical small colony of *Lissoclinum perforatum*. Pembrokeshire.

Lissoclinum weigelei
Lafargue, 1968

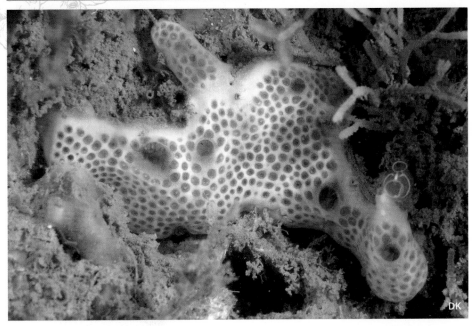

Lissoclinum weigelei with brown zooids and reduced spicule density around the oral openings. Pembrokeshire.

A spiculose didemnid that has only been recently recorded in Britain and Ireland. Superficially similar to *L. perforatum*, it can be distinguished by the presence of brown zooids that give a characteristic brown tinge to the colony. The brown colour seems to outline each of the inhalant pores, though not the larger cloacal openings. The density of spicules is reduced close to the inhalant pores and overall it has an almost dusty appearance.

KEY FEATURES
- White colonies with a brown tinge as a result of brown zooids.
- Reduced spicule density immediately around the inhalant pores.

SIMILAR TO Most similar to *L. perforatum*, which is pure white. Similar to other spiculose didemnids but *Lissoclinum* species have a different zooid density and typically clean-edged pores.

DISTRIBUTION:
Scattered: has been reported from several locations (Scotland, Pembrokeshire, Isle of Man and the Scillies) in Britain and Ireland and is likely to be heavily under-recorded.

ABUNDANCE:
Rare

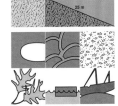

Lissoclinum weigelei alongside a small patch of white *L. perforatum* (top right) for comparison. Isles of Scilly, Cornwall.

Polysyncraton bilobatum
Lafargue, 1968

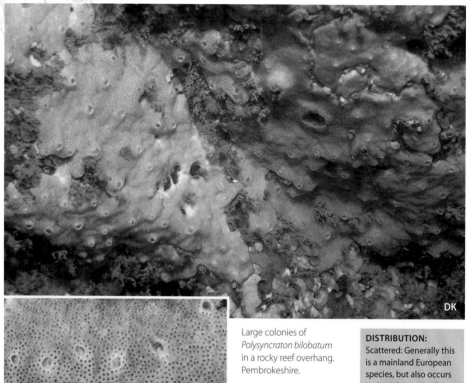

Large colonies of *Polysyncraton bilobatum* in a rocky reef overhang. Pembrokeshire.

Polysyncraton bilobatum. Pembrokeshire.

DISTRIBUTION: Scattered: Generally this is a mainland European species, but also occurs in the Atlantic, English Channel and the North Sea. Has recently been recorded from Pembrokeshire and Norfolk.

ABUNDANCE: Rare

A spiculose didemnid that has only recently been recorded in Britain and Ireland. Abundant and widespread in those locations where it is found, it seems likely that it has a wider distribution around Britain and Ireland. It is characterised by forming very large patches, with a distinctive orange-yellow or apricot coloration. The inhalant pores are regularly spaced with very obvious raised-up white starry points. As with other *Polysyncraton* species, the cloacal openings have pale rims with prominent inward-pointing white 'teeth' at their edge. Found on solid substrates or on kelp holdfasts, it appears to prefer sheltered, reasonably light conditions and so is often seen in shallow water.

KEY FEATURES
- Forms large patches.
- Distinctive orange-yellow or apricot coloration.
- White 'teeth' immediately within the cloacal openings.

SIMILAR TO Similar to other didemnid species, but *P. bilobatum* forms large sheets, has a characteristic colour, and has the distinctive cloacal 'teeth' that are a feature of *Polysyncraton* species.

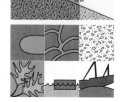

Polysyncraton lacazei
(Giard, 1872)

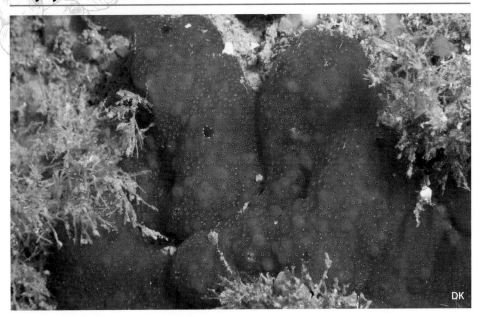

Polysyncraton lacazei with characteristic lumpy appearance. Sark, Channel Islands.

A spiculose didemnid that forms extensive sheets attached to bedrock and has a slightly lumpy appearance. Pink/orange to deep red in colour, it has been described as resembling raspberry jam smeared over the rock. As with other *Polysyncraton* species, the cloacal openings have pale rims with very distinctive inward-pointing white 'teeth' at their edge. Most observations have been from sheltered areas, often where there are maerl or *Zostera* beds, but has also been recorded on current-swept reefs. It appears to favour well-lit areas.

KEY FEATURES
- Characteristic lumpy appearance.
- Pink/orange to deep red in colour, and with prominent white 'teeth' around the cloacal openings.

SIMILAR TO *P. bilobatum* has the same white teeth around the cloacal openings, but lacks the lumpy appearance and is a pale orange colour. *Didemnum pseudofulgens* is a similar red/orange colour but lacks the cloacal 'teeth'.

DISTRIBUTION:
Restricted or localised distribution: predominantly a Mediterranean species, but has now extended northwards to the Channel Isles.

ABUNDANCE:
Rare

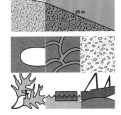

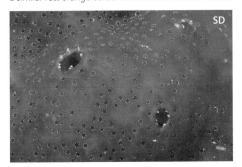

Polysyncraton lacazei with white projections visible around the edge of the cloacal openings. Sark, Channel Islands.

SB

PB

Above: three-dimensional growth of *Trididemnum cereum*. Pembrokeshire.

Left: *Trididemnum cereum* can grow in a lobulose form that may cause confusion with *Didemnum vexillum*. Loch Fyne, Argyll and Bute.

A spiculose didemnid that forms extensive, loosely-attached sheets with a three-dimensional hummocky, wrinkled appearance. Colonies may become free hanging, growing out from their support. Colonies are a mottled, dirty off-white or beige in colour as a result of variable pigment within the animal. The cloacal openings are irregularly spaced, usually on the raised parts of the colony. Generally found on the lower shore and in relatively shallow water.

KEY FEATURES
- Dirty off-white or beige in colour.
- Hummocky and wrinkled appearance.

SIMILAR TO *Didemnum maculosum* is superficially similar, but has a more obvious two-tone coloration. Pale versions could be confused with *Lissoclinum perforatum* or *L. weigelei*, but *T. cereum* is more loosely attached to the substrate and has a 'bubbly' appearance, not forming the neat mounds of *Lissoclinum* species. This species has also been confused with *Didemnum vexillum* on account of the lobulose form and pale colouring. However, *D. vexillum* has no pigment variation at all so lacks the mottled overall appearance.

DISTRIBUTION:
Scattered

ABUNDANCE:
Occasional

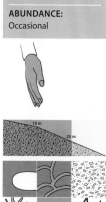

Distaplia rosea with only the upper surface visible. Pembrokeshire.

DISTRIBUTION:
Scattered: all round Britain and Ireland from southern Scotland southwards, but likely to be under-recorded.

ABUNDANCE:
Occasional

Distaplia rosea in a habitat with less sediment, revealing the stalks of each head. Strangford Lough, Co. Down.

This species forms colonies of small dome-shaped lobes with a very characteristic pink colour (hence *rosea*). Often found in silty conditions with only the upper surface of the colony visible. Zooids are completely embedded in a transparent test with small flecks of white colour giving the colony a spangled appearance. Typically found in sheltered muddy areas where there are rocks, shells or reef on which to attach.

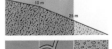

KEY FEATURES
• Small colonies with a characteristic transparent pinkish appearance.

SIMILAR TO The distinctive pink colour and cushioned appearance mean *D. rosea* is unlikely to be mistaken for any other British species. *Botryllus schlosseri* can occasionally be found in small pink patches, but has a pronounced star-like arrangement of zooids.

Archidistoma aggregatum Garstang, 1891

'Bunch of grapes' appearance of *Archidistoma aggregatum*. Pembrokeshire.

This inconspicuous compound sea squirt consists of small globular heads on short stalks. Each head comprises around ten zooids, each of which has both oral and atrial openings visible (unlike for example in *Aplidium* species, where multiple zooids share a common cloacal opening). Colonies are almost colourless, with a brown or grey overall hue and no obvious markings, and are sometimes lightly encrusted with sand. Overall, each head has a bumpy appearance, somewhat reminiscent of a small bunch of grapes. Normally found in scoured areas with significant tidal streams.

KEY FEATURES
- Globular heads on short stalks, with an overall lumpy appearance.
- Largely colourless but may have a slight brown, olive green or yellowish hue.
- Zooids, although partially embedded in test, have independent exhalant openings as opposed to sharing a common cloacal opening.

DISTRIBUTION:
Scattered: from southern Scotland and Northern Ireland southwards, although probably under-recorded owing to its inconspicuous appearance and small size.

ABUNDANCE:
Occasional

SIMILAR TO *Perophora listeri* and *Pycnoclavella producta* have separate zooids connected by a stolon, as opposed to being fused together.

Left: zooids of *A. aggregatum* have two visible openings ('di-stoma') and do not share a common cloacal opening. Pembrokeshire.

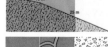

Aplidium cf. *glabrum* (Verrill, 1871)

Aplidium cf. *glabrum*. Milford Haven, Pembrokeshire.

There is significant confusion regarding this species, and it seems likely that the name has been used to refer to several different species; caution should thus be applied when interpreting the recording data. This name is currently used in Europe to describe what is believed to be a non-native species. In Dutch it has the vernacular name 'glanzende bolzakpijp' meaning 'glossy ball bagpipe' (the Dutch word 'zakpijp' being used for both sea squirt and bagpipe). However, this does not appear to be the same species as the one originally described as *A. glabrum* by Verrill (1871), which is a northern species. Further work will be required to resolve these confusions.

For the purposes of this guide, *Aplidium* cf. *glabrum* is a compound species that forms somewhat featureless colonies with a shiny grey appearance. The zooids can be seen through the semi-translucent test. It is generally found, as are many non-native sea squirts, attached to artificial substrates in marinas and sheltered silty environments.

KEY FEATURES
- Forms grey, translucent and shiny colonies with visible zooids.
- Overall colony appearance is that of an irregular and featureless mound.

SIMILAR TO *A. nordmanni* can show a grey-white coloration, but has much more striking white pigmentation of the zooids. *A. pallidum* is similarly featureless but grows as multiple small colonies, usually on algae.

DISTRIBUTION:
Scattered: found in the Netherlands in 1977, and has been recorded from Lancashire, south to Milford Haven around to the coast of Norfolk. It is unclear if the records from northern British and Irish waters are the same species.

ABUNDANCE:
Occasional

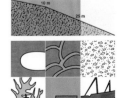

Aplidium nordmanni (Milne Edwards, 1841)

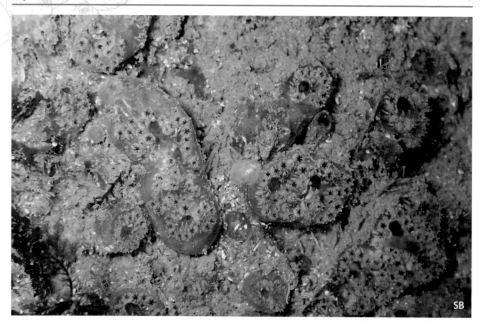

This is a very distinctive species that forms flat-topped fleshy colonies with steep edges and openings only on the upper surface, never on the sides. It usually has a pink-red coloration, but can also be found in white (see page 18). Zooids are heavily pigmented in white and the colonies have conspicuous cloacal openings. Oral openings have six outward-facing papillae. Generally prefers exposed conditions and clearer water.

Above: multiple colonies of *Aplidium nordmanni*. Pembrokeshire.

KEY FEATURES
- Thick, flat topped colonies with distinct opening-free sides.
- Red or white coloration with heavily pigmented zooids and prominent cloacal openings.

SIMILAR TO *Botryllus schlosseri* and *Botrylloides leachii* form thinner sheets. *Aplidium elegans* forms thick colonies but with a more rounded growth form, and with zooid openings all over the surface of the mass, as opposed to solely on the top face in the

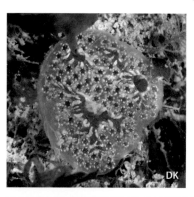

case of *A. nordmanni*. *A. elegans* also has eight very visible outward-facing papillae around each oral opening, whereas *A. nordmanni* has only six. It is unclear if *A. nordmanni* is a separate species from what is described as *A. proliferum* in some texts.

Aplidium nordmanni showing six papillae around each oral opening. Pembrokeshire.

DISTRIBUTION:
Scattered: predominantly in the Irish Sea and the west coast of Scotland.

ABUNDANCE:
Frequent

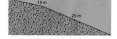

Aplidium ocellatum

Aplidium ocellatum. Swanage Bay, Dorset.

This compound species superficially resembles a pale, transparent *Morchellium argus* on a shorter stalk. Each zooid has a very distinctive white pigment ring around the oral siphon, and two small red dots immediately underneath the rim. This species appears to be at the northernmost limit of its distribution, with British and Irish records so far limited to the Channel Isles and the south coast, as far west as the Isles of Scilly.

DISTRIBUTION:
Restricted or localised distribution: northern France, the Channel Isles, the Isles of Scilly and along the south coast.

ABUNDANCE:
Occasional

KEY FEATURES
- Colonies of club-shaped heads.
- A distinctive white ring on each zooid.

SIMILAR TO *Morchellium argus* has a similar overall zooid arrangement but lacks the distinctive white rings of *A. ocellatum*.

Aplidium ocellatum. Sark, Channel Islands.

Aplidium pallidum (Verrill, 1871)

Aplidium pallidum on algae. Fal Estuary, Cornwall.

This species forms multiple small cushion-like masses. Zooids are indistinct, with the colonies having a soft clean jelly-like appearance, yellowish-buff in colour. Typically found on rock and especially on algae or *Zostera*, it favours areas of moderate exposure and tidal streams. In tidal channels, it can commonly be found attached to the seaweed *Halidrys siliquosa*.

KEY FEATURES
- Multiple small jelly-like masses, yellowish-buff, commonly on algae.

SIMILAR TO *Aplidium* cf. *glabrum* forms larger cushions, typically found singly.

DISTRIBUTION:
Scattered: south and west coasts of Britain and Ireland.

ABUNDANCE:
Occasional

Aplidium pallidum. Sark, Channel Islands.

Aplidium punctum (Giard, 1873)

Aplidium punctum. Sark, Channel Islands.

This species forms colonies of neat, club-shaped heads with a well-developed stalk that is usually visible. The head consists of closely packed greyish zooids, each with a single bright orange spot. The overall impression is of a pinky-orange glow coming from within each head. Very common in areas of considerable water movement, typical of vertical rock faces in shallow water. Can also be found on stones and shells to a depth of over 20m.

DISTRIBUTION:
Widespread

ABUNDANCE:
Abundant

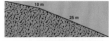

Aplidium punctum on a vertical reef face. Pembrokeshire.

Aplidium punctum showing a single bright orange dot per zooid and the cloacal opening at the top of the head. Pembrokeshire.

KEY FEATURES
- Colonies of club-shaped heads with a single orange spot on each zooid (see above).

SIMILAR TO *Morchellium argus* also forms colonies of club-like heads, but has four red spots on each zooid, a background colour that is more candyfloss pink than orange, and a 'folded' appearance.

Aplidium 'strawberry'

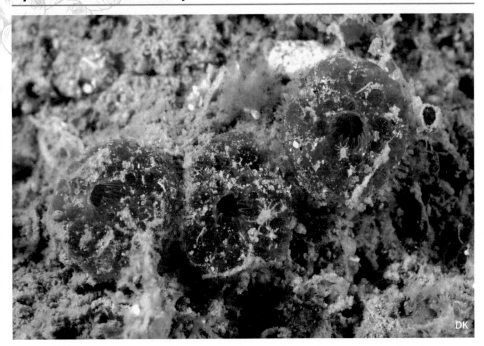

Aplidium 'strawberry' showing prominent projections around the central cloacal openings. Pembrokeshire.

This is a very distinctive compound species consisting of small flat-topped lobes with zooids arranged around a central cloacal opening. It has a distinctive red-orange colour, and almost always seems to occur in small groups of individual lobes as opposed to extensive sheets. On close inspection, long projections (languets) can be seen surrounding the cloacal opening. This species is currently undescribed.

KEY FEATURES
• Bright red-orange flat-topped lobes.
• Long projections around the cloacal opening.

SIMILAR TO Small colonies of the red version of *A. nordmanni* may look similar but always have additional white markings, where *A.* 'strawberry' is a single uniform colour.

DISTRIBUTION:
Restricted or localised distribution: Irish Sea from Pembrokeshire to as far north as Rathlin Island and Strangford Lough.

ABUNDANCE:
Occasional

Multiple lobes of *Aplidium* 'strawberry'. Isle of Man.

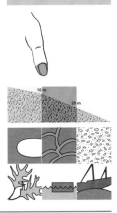

Morchellium argus (Milne Edwards, 1841)

Loose folded appearance of heads of *Morchellium argus*. Isle of Man.

A compound species forming colonies of globular heads that are pinkish in colour and attached to the substrate by short stalks. The zooids are grouped in such a way as to give the impression of darker grooves dividing each head into segments, resulting in an overall 'folded' appearance. If visible, the stalk is pale orange-red in colour and usually encrusted with sand. Each individual zooid has four red spots arranged around the oral opening. Generally found in areas with moderate to strong water movement, often beneath overhangs or on vertical rock faces.

KEY FEATURES
- Pinkish heads having a well-defined stalk and a loose, folded appearance.
- Each zooid has four small red spots.

SIMILAR TO *Aplidium punctum* is a similar stalked species, but the stalk is clean and more readily visible in *A. punctum*, and each zooid has only one spot, as opposed to four in *M. argus*. The overall appearance of *A. punctum* is neater, rather than the looser, folded appearance of *M. argus*.

DISTRIBUTION:
Widespread

ABUNDANCE:
Abundant

Above: the stalks of *Morchellium argus* are often encrusted with sand. Pembrokeshire.

Left: four red dots per zooid. Strangford Lough, Co. Down.

Polyclinum aurantium Milne Edwards, 1841

Polyclinum aurantium. St Kilda.

Polyclinum aurantium partially encrusted with algae. North Rona.

DISTRIBUTION:
Widespread

ABUNDANCE:
Frequent

A highly variable compound species that forms small rounded colonies, typically dirty yellow to olive green in colour, and sometimes a more golden yellow. Favours exposed places such as surge gullies, and is often found attached to kelp stipes or on rock. Often encrusted with sand, although typically cleaner in more tide-swept offshore locations where there is little sand or silt.

KEY FEATURES
- Forms mounds with irregularly arranged zooids and multiple cloacal openings.
- Often has sand, algae or other detritus attached.

SIMILAR TO Small colonies of *Synoicum pulmonaria* (not described in this publication) are similar and can only be reliably distinguished by examination of the internal anatomy. *Archidistoma aggregatum* has a similar lumpy appearance but is much less conspicuous, and again lacks the yellow colour. See also separate entry on sand-encrusted polyclinids pages 67–68.

Aplidium elegans (Giard, 1872)

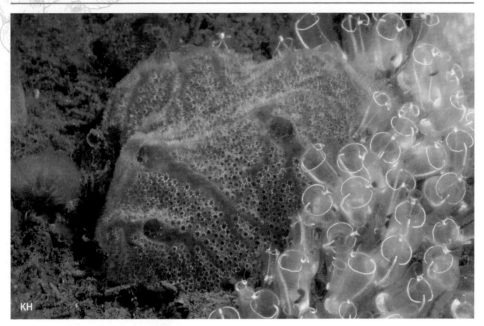

Above: *Aplidium elegans* with *Clavelina lepadiformis*. Plymouth, Devon.
Below: *Aplidium elegans* with eight papillae around each oral opening. Falmouth, Cornwall.

A visually striking compound species that forms reddish-pink cushions or small balls with white markings around the oral openings. Zooids have their oral openings over the entire surface of the colony, including down the sides, and are ringed with eight prominent white papillae. They are arranged in a meandering pattern, with canals leading between the cloacal openings. Found in rocky sites, usually with moderate tidal streams.

KEY FEATURES
- Forms firm, cushion-like masses of reddish-pink and white.
- Eight prominent white papillae around the inhalant pores, giving a spiky appearance.

SIMILAR TO The most likely confusion is with the red form of *Aplidium nordmanni*. The latter, however, has flat-topped colonies with sides that are free of oral openings, and siphons fringed with six as opposed to eight papillae.

DISTRIBUTION:
Scattered: generally a southern species

ABUNDANCE:
Frequent

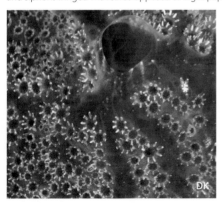

NOTE Older sources refer to this and *A. turbinatum* as *Sidnyum*. It should be noted that in British and Irish waters, *Aplidium* species have only six papillae around each zooid opening, whereas those previously called *Sidnyum* have eight.

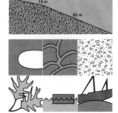

Aplidium turbinatum (Savigny, 1816)

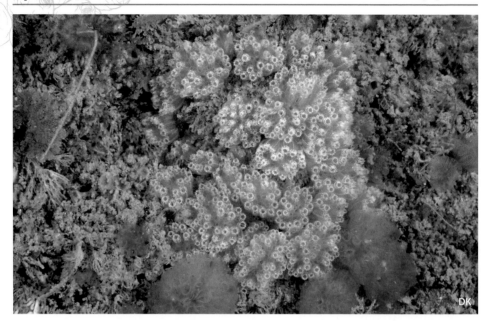

Aplidium turbinatum. Pembrokeshire.

A small compound species, with each lobe formed of zooids arranged in a single ring around a central cloacal opening (a system). Several lobes may be found clustered together to form a colony, but remain separate and not fused into a larger sheet. Lobes are transparent with white pigmentation on the top and in ribs down the sides of each zooid. Each oral siphon has eight papillae around the rim. Typically found on steep rock faces or around kelp holdfasts in relatively shallow water.

KEY FEATURES
- Small single-system lobes that taper slightly towards the base.
- Extensive white pigment around the tops and sides of the siphons with eight papillae around the rim.

SIMILAR TO *A. turbinatum* could be confused with small colonies of the white form of *Aplidium nordmanni*, but the latter is opaque and has a more swollen appearance. The eight papillae around each siphon is a diagnostic feature that also helps to tell them apart. Most other *Aplidium* species have only six (see note to *A. elegans* on previous page).

DISTRIBUTION:
Widespread

ABUNDANCE:
Frequent

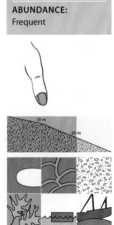

Eight papillae around the oral opening of each zooid of *Aplidium turbinatum*. Pembrokeshire.

Sand-encrusted polyclinids

There are several morphologically distinct sand-encrusted polyclinids in British and Irish waters. Some have flat-topped lobes comprising usually just a single system, whereas others have a more rounded shape with multiple systems and cloacal openings. One form that has been photographed in the Isles of Scilly is characterised by a regular arrangement of paired zooids radiating out from the centre. Where visible, the background colour of the test can be grey through to orange, and in some instances the inhalant pores are ringed with black pigment. Some examples are illustrated in this section.

Although definitive identification can be made by examination of the internal anatomy, more work is needed to reliably match these field characteristics to individual species. At the present time, the candidate species for a sand-encrusted polyclinid would include *Aplidium densum*, *Aplidium* 'honeycomb', *Polyclinum aurantium*, *Synoicum incrustatum* and possibly others.

Aplidium densum forms cushions with a single cloacal opening, and the side and upper surface encrusted with sand.

Aplidium 'honeycomb' is characterised by having flat-topped lobes closely pressed together with sand coated sides. The honeycomb pattern of zooids has a brown/beige colour. Note that Habitas website (see page 195) shows a picture of this species (incorrectly) in the entry for *Aplidium glabrum*.

Polyclinum aurantium (see separate entry on page 64) forms larger lumps that show a less regular zooid arrangement and multiple cloacal openings, and is often golden in colour. Under certain conditions it can be heavily encrusted with sand.

Synoicum incrustatum has been recorded (Connor, 1989) on the north coast of Ireland. This compound species is a grey or grey-brown colour, with individual lobes tightly clustered on the substrate and heavily encrusted with sand. Each lobe is flat-topped, with zooids arranged around a central cloacal opening, typically just one, although larger lobes may have more. Favours areas with strong tidal streams and a certain amount of sand scour.

Given the uncertainty in matching field appearance to species, it is recommended that such observations are recorded as 'sand encrusted polyclinid'.

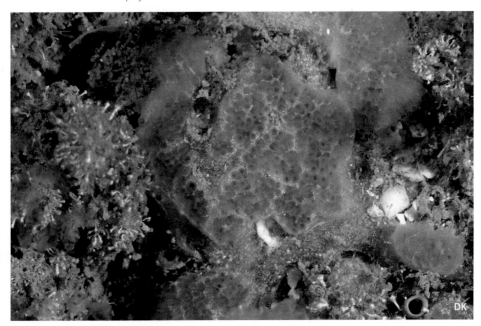

Flat-topped lobes of *Aplidium* 'honeycomb' with embedded sand. Pembrokeshire.

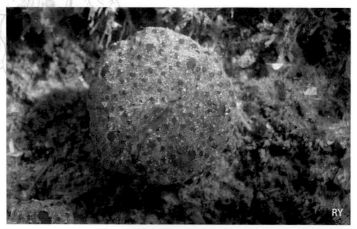

Left: Devon.

Right: Pembrokeshire.

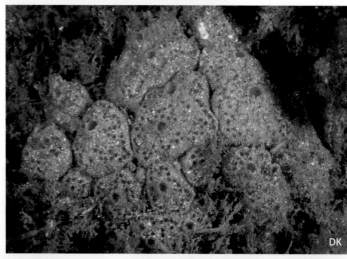

Pembrokeshire.

Isles of Scilly, Cornwall.

Ascidia conchilega

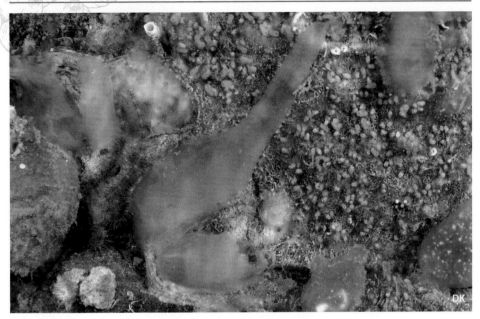

Ascidia conchilega with a prominent, elongated oral siphon, amongst other unitary sea squirts. Lough Hyne, Co. Cork.

This unitary sea squirt is irregularly shaped and conforms to the space available. Greenish in colour, the thin translucent test is easily torn and often has small rough projections over the surface. The siphons are located far apart on the body, with the oral siphon capable of great extension. Each siphon is marked with small red spots; eight around the oral and six around the atrial. It is generally found between or underneath boulders or in rock crevices, attached to the substrate by most of the left side, often with only the oral siphon visible.

KEY FEATURES

- Unitary sea squirt with an elongate, oval-shaped body that is translucent and greenish.
- Oral siphon is located at the end of the animal and the atrial siphon about two-thirds of the way down the body.
- Both siphons have small red dots around the edges.

SIMILAR TO *A. mentula* can be greyish when found under overhangs, but the white 'teeth' around the siphons and the thicker pink-to-grey test distinguishes it from *A. conchilega*.

DISTRIBUTION:
Widespread with a bias:
to western coasts

ABUNDANCE:
Frequent

Ascidia conchilega with greenish internal coloration. Lough Hyne, Co. Cork.

Ascidia mentula

Müller, 1776

Ascidia mentula in a small reef overhang. Loch Sunart, Highland.

A large, unitary sea squirt with an elongated oval-shaped body attached along its left side to the substrate. The test is thick, and ranges in colour from deep red in well-lit locations, through pink, to grey with tiny red/pink spots when found in dark overhangs. It is often heavily overgrown and obscured by detritus. Siphons are wide but short, with the oral siphon at one end and the atrial siphon positioned halfway along the body. A distinctive feature is a number of small white teeth-like projections around the edge of each siphon; these are readily visible in red individuals, although somewhat harder to see in grey animals. Typically found on vertical or overhanging rock faces. In suitable habitats, numerous individuals may be found together. It is host to several commensal species, such as the bivalve *Musculus subpictus*.

DISTRIBUTION:
Widespread

ABUNDANCE:
Abundant

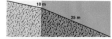

The white 'teeth' and siphon position of *Ascidia mentula*. Pembrokeshire.

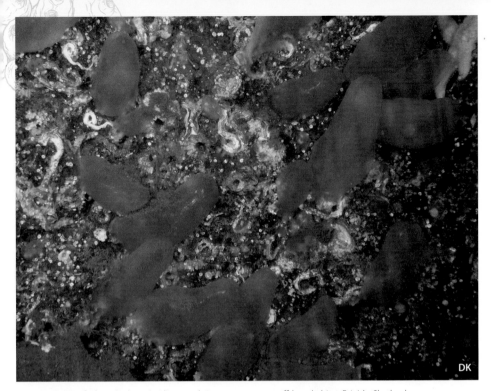

An aggregation of relatively clean *Ascidia mentula* in a current-swept offshore habitat. Fair Isle, Shetland.

KEY FEATURES

- A large unitary species with a thick red to grey test, often heavily overgrown.
- Characteristic white 'teeth', particularly obvious around the oral siphon.

SIMILAR TO The white projections around the siphons distinguish *A. mentula* from other unitary sea squirts, the most similar being *A. conchilega*, which is green in colour and has small red spots around the siphons, and *A. virginea*, which has a clean, translucent rose-pink test.

A pale *Ascidia mentula* with white 'teeth' around both siphons. Oban, Argyll and Bute.

Different colour variants of *Ascidia virginea*. Isle of Skye, Highland.

A heavily mottled *Ascidia virginea*. Loch Nevis, Highland.

DISTRIBUTION:
Widespread with a bias: mainly found in the north of Britain and Ireland

ABUNDANCE:
Frequent

A unitary sea squirt with a thick, translucent pale pink or milky-white test that is very clean in appearance and does not contract when disturbed. The depth of colour is very variable and sometimes there is a mottled pattern on the body. Animals are roughly rectangular in shape, and attach upright to the substrate by a small area of the base. The oral siphon is at the top of the animal, with the atrial siphon around quarter of the way down the side. It is found on rocky substrates in sheltered or semi-exposed silty conditions, and very occasionally in aggregations (e.g. in some Scottish sea lochs).

KEY FEATURES
• A unitary species with a clean pinkish test, attached by the base.
SIMILAR TO *Corella parallelogramma* has a clean transparent test with very distinctive coloured internal markings. *Ciona intestinalis* has yellow rims on the siphons and contracts strongly when disturbed.

Ascidiella aspersa Fluted Sea Squirt (Müller, 1776)

A dense aggregation of *Ascidiella aspersa*. Loch Sunart, Highland.

Ascidiella aspersa. Loch Torridon, Highland.

A tall oval unitary sea squirt with a grey, semi-transparent test found attached to the substrate by its base. It has a rough surface that is often covered with lightly-adhering detritus. The siphons are fluted, and the atrial siphon is situated about one third of the way down the body and angled upwards. Both siphons have a series of lighter markings around them. This species can be present in large numbers in suitable habitats, and favours shallow sheltered sites including harbours and sea lochs. It is often found in clumps attached to algae and to shells or pebbles on mud. Often it will be one of the first species to re-colonise an area after dredging.

KEY FEATURES
- Grey and semi-transparent with a dirty rough surface.
- Typically sits upright, attached at the base.
- Fluted siphons.

SIMILAR TO *A. scabra* is smaller, with a rounder overall shape and is attached by its side.

DISTRIBUTION:
Widespread

ABUNDANCE:
Abundant

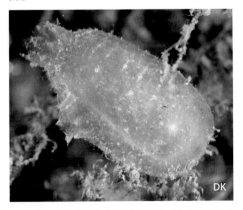

Ascidiella aspersa. Strangford Lough, Co. Down.

Ascidiella scabra

(Müller, 1776)

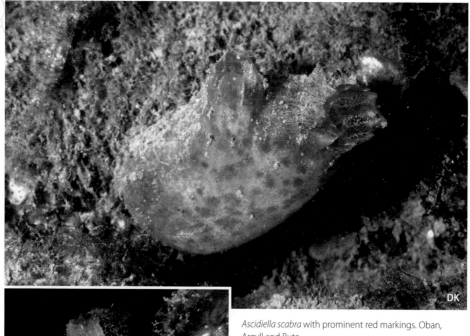

Ascidiella scabra with prominent red markings. Oban, Argyll and Bute.

Ascidiella scabra showing relative siphon positions. Isle of Skye, Highland.

DISTRIBUTION:
Widespread: particularly common in Scottish sea lochs

ABUNDANCE:
Abundant

A small sea squirt usually found attached along one side, with the siphons appearing to be at the same level, about a quarter of the body length apart. Colour is variable and individuals usually show some red markings. Siphons typically have cream and red longitudinal stripes. It is found in sheltered locations with some current, often attached to other sea squirts, bryozoans or algae.

KEY FEATURES
- Grey and semi-transparent with some cream and red markings.
- Siphons appear to be at the same level, quarter of the body length apart.

SIMILAR TO *A. aspersa* is taller and more upright, with the atrial siphon about a third of the way down the side of the body and angled upwards, whereas *A. scabra* is more rounded and appears to be lying on its side.

Phallusia mammillata (Cuvier, 1815)

The largest unitary sea squirt in British and Irish waters, *Phallusia mammillata*. Lyme Bay, Devon/Dorset.

The largest British unitary sea squirt, it has a thick, cartilaginous test covered in bumps and ridges. The shape is that of a plump bottle; pale grey, brownish or milky white in colour. Smaller specimens have a distinctive blueish tinge. It generally prefers warm, sheltered areas where there is little water movement (such as in harbours and on pontoons), but can be found in open water sites with more water movement, such as Lyme Bay.

KEY FEATURES
- Large grey/brownish/white species with prominent bumps and ridges.
- Distinctive flask or bottle-like shape.

SIMILAR TO No other sea squirt in British and Irish waters resembles this species.

DISTRIBUTION:
Restricted or localised distribution: restricted to the south and south-west of the geographical area; common in the far south-west of Ireland (Bantry Bay) but rare elsewhere

ABUNDANCE:
Frequent

Phallusia mammillata.
Lyme Bay, Devon/Dorset.

Ciona intestinalis Yellow-ringed Sea Squirt (Linnaeus, 1767)

Ciona intestinalis with visible sperm duct. Loch Nevis, Highland.

A dense aggregation of *Ciona intestinalis*. Loch Hourn, Highland.

A large unitary sea squirt with a soft gelatinous cylindrical body attached to the substrate by its base, and long siphons close together at the upper end. The body is semi-transparent in young specimens, becoming more opaque in adults, yellowish-green to sometimes orange-brown in colour. The whole body is highly contractile when disturbed. There are characteristic yellow markings around the rim of each siphon, usually appearing as a continuous, scalloped line but sometimes broken into separate markings or even totally absent in some specimens. Small red spots (light-sensing organs) are visible on the siphon rims. It can be abundant in sheltered areas with some current, particularly on man-made structures such as wrecks, jetties, buoys and ropes. It can also be found in moderately exposed shallow locations, but usually as single specimens rather than in groups.

DISTRIBUTION:
Widespread

ABUNDANCE:
Abundant

KEY FEATURES
- Tall cylindrical body that contracts strongly when disturbed.
- Usually with yellow markings and small red spots around the rims of both siphons, although the yellow can be broken or absent.

SIMILAR TO Adult *C. intestinalis* are unlikely to be mistaken for other species given their distinctive yellow markings, soft texture and highly contractile behaviour. Young

specimens are more transparent than adults, and might be confused with small individuals of *Corella parallelogramma*, although the latter has a more rectangular shape, lacks the yellow siphon rims, and has a rigid non-contractile body.

Variable yellow pigmentation on *Ciona intestinalis* individuals. Loch Long, Argyll and Bute.

Corella eumyota Orange-tipped Sea Squirt Traustedt, 1882

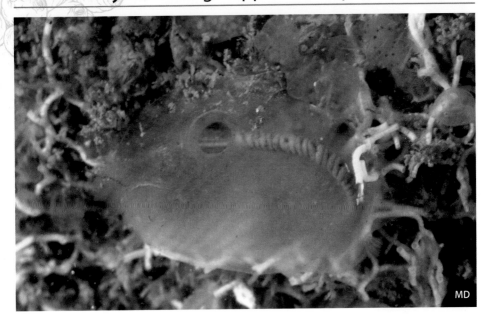

MD

Corella eumyota with spiral faecal matter. Isle of Wight.

A small unitary sea squirt with a smooth, rigid and semi-translucent tunic, found attached along one side of its body. Overall, the body is off-white to orange in colour, with older individuals often having orange pigmentation around the two very short siphons. As with *C. parallelogramma*, it has a C-shaped gut that is visible through the test and runs along the edge of the body. Within the gut the faecal rope is wound into an ordered spiral, giving the gut contents a distinctive spring-like appearance. This is a non-native species that is generally found in harbours and marinas attached to man-made structures, although it can also be found in shallow and sheltered natural habitats and beneath boulders on the shore.

KEY FEATURES
- Smooth and semi-translucent, generally lying flat and having a characteristic rounded dent in the centre of the body.
- Short siphons often with orange coloration.
- C-shaped gut runs along edge of body and contains distinctive spiral faecal matter.

SIMILAR TO *C. parallelogramma* is upright and transparent, has patches of coloured pigment inside the body, and lacks the spiral gut contents. *Ascidiella aspersa* has a rougher tunic, and an S-shaped gut that meanders through the middle of the body, whereas the gut is C-shaped and runs along the edge of the body in *C. eumyota*.

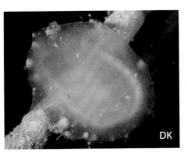

DK

Corella eumyota with C-shaped gut. Strangford Lough, Co. Down.

DISTRIBUTION:
Scattered: First recorded in Britain and Ireland in 2004, it is now found in open water locations on the south coast and as far north as Northumberland and Rathlin Island, as well as in harbours as far north as Orkney

ABUNDANCE:
Frequent

Corella parallelogramma Gas Mantle Sea Squirt (Müller, 1776)

Corella parallelogramma with non-pigmented branchial sac. Isle of Skye, Highland.

Corella parallelogramma with pigmented 'gas mantle' branchial sac. Loch Hourn, Highland.

A unitary sea squirt that is rectangular in shape, laterally flattened, and attached by the base. It is transparent, with the branchial sac and other internal organs clearly visible, and has an L-shaped gut that runs along the bottom and up one side of the body. Pigmentation of the internal organs can be variable but usually forms a criss-cross pattern, flecked with white, yellow and red. It is found in a wide range of habitats and conditions, often where there is some water movement, and generally as scattered individuals.

KEY FEATURES
- Flattened rectangular shape, upright appearance.
- Transparent with internal markings in white and red, sometimes but not always showing a 'gas mantle' effect.
- L-shaped gut along edge of body.

SIMILAR TO No other species is the same shape and as transparent as *C. parallelogramma*. *Ascidiella scabra* can be partially transparent and show red and white markings, but is attached by its side and has a meandering S-shaped gut. *C. eumyota* is less transparent, attaches by its side, and has a distinctive spiral packing of the faecal rope in the gut. Young *Ciona intestinalis* specimens can be transparent and show a faint 'gas mantle' effect, but are elongated and cylindrical in shape and highly contractile when disturbed.

DISTRIBUTION:
Widespread with a bias: bias to the west coast of Scotland/Northern Ireland

ABUNDANCE:
Abundant

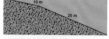

An aggregation of *Corella parallelogramma*. Loch Etive, Argyll and Bute.

Perophora japonica Creeping Sea Squirt

SB

Perophora japonica growing over algae. Fal Estuary, Cornwall.

Yellow star-shaped buds at the end of the stolons of *Perophora japonica*. Fal Estuary, Cornwall.

DK

DISTRIBUTION:
Scattered: This is a non-native species that was originally restricted to the south coast of England, with records from Plymouth, Dorset, Guernsey and the Helford river, but now has been recorded as far north as N Devon, Norfolk and Strangford Lough.

ABUNDANCE:
Occasional

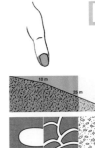

This is a stoloniferous species, composed of small transparent zooids linked by a creeping stolon. This, together with the native *P. listeri*, are the only two British sea squirts where a basal stolon is readily visible. Individual zooids have a rounded rectangular shape and are strikingly greenish-yellow in colour, with the gut visible inside. The growth habit consists of zooids connected to the stolon by short stalks, giving a dense, bushy appearance. Characteristic yellow star-shaped buds at the ends of the stolons are distinctive. Colonies are found growing in patches attached to solid surfaces in shallow and sheltered water, typically harbours, marinas and associated with bivalve aquaculture. It is also increasingly found in natural habitats. Grows vigorously, and often over other sessile organisms.

KEY FEATURES
- Transparent pillow-like zooids connected by creeping stolons.
- Greenish-yellow in colour with bright yellow star-shaped 'buds' at the end of the stolons.

SIMILAR TO *P. listeri* lacks the bright yellow stars and is not as vividly greenish-yellow in colour, with zooids organised more loosely.

Perophora listeri

Wiegman, 1835

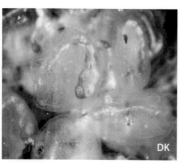

Perophora listeri growing around the base of the hydroid *Nemertesia antennina*. Strangford Lough, Co. Down.

Perophora listeri with visible stolons, growing on algae. Pembrokeshire.

This is a small and inconspicuous species, composed of small transparent zooids linked by a creeping stolon. This and the non-native *P. japonica* are the only two British sea squirts where a basal stolon is readily visible. Individual zooids have a rounded, rectangular shape, often with a faint green coloration. It often forms irregular lines of zooids creeping over the substrate, attached to the stolon by stalks. The overall effect is of a loose, irregular arrangement of the zooids. Tolerant of silty conditions, it will grow over a range of substrates including hydroids, algae and even crabs. Generally found in relatively sheltered locations.

KEY FEATURES

- Tiny transparent pillow-like zooids connected by a creeping stolon that is sometimes visible.
- Clear to slightly green in colour, forms loosely arranged colonies that creep over the substrate.
- Ovoid faecal pellets readily visible within the zooid.

SIMILAR TO *P. japonica* forms tighter colonies, typically a brighter greenish-yellow with characteristic terminal yellow stars. *Pycnoclavella producta* is also transparent and lacks pigmentation, but grows in a more ordered and upright fashion in habitats with a greater degree of water movement.

DISTRIBUTION:
Scattered: probably under-recorded

ABUNDANCE:
Frequent

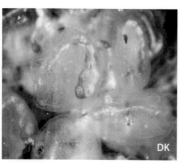

The gut of *Perophora listeri* has a characteristic shape and colour. Pembrokeshire.

80 SEA SQUIRTS

Molgulids

Molgulids are unitary sea squirts having ovoid or ball-shaped bodies with both siphons on the top. One feature that distinguishes the molgulids from other British unitary sea squirts is the presence of six upright, pointed papillae around the oral siphon, resembling a cartoon crown. This distinctive feature is clearly visible when the animal is seen from the side, even in very small specimens.

There are a substantial number of European molgulid species (see Monniot, 1969) and the potential for mis-identification is high. The molgulids are a very difficult group to identify *in situ* because they generally lack sufficient external features that can be used to make a definitive identification. This is made even more problematic by many species being found buried in sediment with only their siphons visible, thus giving even less information to aid identification. Indeed, many molgulids can only be confidently identified by dissection and examination of their internal anatomy.

At least three species live embedded in coarse gravel, sand or muddy sand (*Molgula occulta*, *Molgula oculata* and *Eugyra arenosa*). With experience these can be sometimes be distinguished based on their *in situ* appearance, with *M. oculata* perhaps the most distinctive in that it lives in coarse shell gravel and can maintain a bare area between the siphons, presumably by contraction and movement of the animal. The remaining sediment-dwelling species can only be identified confidently by examination of their internal anatomy and are best recorded as 'sediment-dwelling molgulid'.

Some surface-dwelling species are found as single individuals (for example *Molgula citrina*, a species character-ised by a semi-transparent grey-green body through which the internal organs can be seen). Others (sometimes termed 'sea grapes') are commonly found in dense aggregations, usually on man-made structures. Although typically recorded (and potentially mis-recorded) as *Molgula manhattensis*, it is possible that many records are in fact *Molgula socialis* or yet another species. With the large number of potential molgulid species and the limited features visible upon which to make an identification, it is recommended that most specimens be recorded as 'molgulid sp.' in the absence of verification by dissection.

Unidentified small *Molgula*. Poole Bay, Dorset.

Molgula sp. Dorset.

Prominent projections around the oral siphon of this gravel-dwelling *Molgula*. Isle of Man.

Some *Molgula* have thin siphons located close together. Pembrokeshire.

Gravel-dwelling *Molgula*. Isle of Man.

Molgula complanata

Sand-encrusted *Molgula complanata* with crown-like projections around the oral siphon, on algae. Pembrokeshire.

A small, sand-encrusted molgulid typically found attached to algae. The body is a flattened ovoid, attached by the base, with very small siphons bearing the characteristic molgulid 'crown' around the oral siphon. The size and sand encrustation make this a very inconspicuous species.

KEY FEATURES

- Molgulid 'crown' around the oral siphon.
- Typically found attached to algae.
- Body is usually completely encrusted with sand.

SIMILAR TO The combination of habitat (algae) and sand encrustation make this an inconspicuous but readily identifiable species.

DISTRIBUTION:
Scattered

ABUNDANCE:
Rare

Multiple *Molgula complanata* on algae. Pembrokeshire.

Boltenia echinata Cactus Sea Squirt (Linnaeus, 1767)

Above: *Boltenia echinata* showing branched surface spines. Firth of Lorn, Argyll and Bute.

Multiple individuals of *Boltenia echinata* on a single *Ascidia mentula*. Firth of Lorn, Argyll and Bute.

DISTRIBUTION:
Restricted or localised distribution: northern species, almost exclusively found in Scotland

ABUNDANCE:
Rare

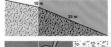

This is a very small, round or oval-shaped species with distinctive radially branched spines on its surface. It is attached by its base, with short siphons on the upper side of the body. These are striped in white and pale orange, and are square when partially closed. The branched spines on the test give it a characteristic spiky appearance and often trap silt. Found attached to hard substrata or to other sea squirts in moderately sheltered silty sites.

KEY FEATURES
- A very small ball-like sea squirt with conspicuous branched spines.
- Pale brownish-cream leathery test with short siphons that are square when partially closed.

SIMILAR TO The diminutive size and surface spines make this a very distinctive species, unlikely to be confused with others.

Bolteniopsis prenanti Harant, 1927

A field of *Bolteniopsis prenanti* in a fragile sponge and anthozoan community. Isles of Scilly, Cornwall.

A small, inconspicuous but readily-identifiable species consisting of an egg-shaped zooid raised from the substrate by a thin stalk that may be as much as ten times the length of the body. The oral siphon is on the top of the zooid with the atrial siphon protruding from the side. The translucent test is usually lightly encrusted with silt and sand. This species can be found on deep rocky areas with sand and silt in the Scillies and Channel Islands but has yet to be recorded from mainland Britain or Ireland.

KEY FEATURES
· Single, small encrusted zooid on a stalk.

SIMILAR TO *Pycnoclavella* spp. zooids are of a similar size and may be somewhat stalked. However, the long stalk and encrusted test of *B. prenanti* should make it relatively easy to identify. *B. prenanti* may also be confused with the stalked sponge *Clathrina lacunosa* but the latter has a ribbed body typical of a sponge and no siphons.

DISTRIBUTION:
Restricted or localised distribution: records from Scillies and the Channel Islands

ABUNDANCE:
Rare

Bolteniopsis prenanti.
Sark, Channel Islands.

Pyura and *Microcosmus*

These two genera of the Pyuridae comprise a group of difficult-to-identify unitary sea squirts with siphons of varying colours, sizes and positions, and usually warty (tessellated) bodies. In this section we discuss *Pyura microcosmus*, *P. tessellata* and *P. squamulosa*, together with *Microcosmus claudicans*. A general description of all four is provided below.

With the limitations of current knowledge, great care is required to identify these to species level in the field, and in some cases this can only be achieved by dissection and inspection of the internal features. There is little mention of colour in the literature apart from Berrill (1950) who states that 'colour among pyurids, though vivid internally and usually drab externally, is notoriously variable'. Body texture may help, but the term 'tessellate' refers to a rough, mosaic-type texture on the body, and whilst this is a good indicator for some, it seems not to be the case for *P. squamulosa*, which is described as 'smooth, with lilac coloured veins' by Berrill.

	Pyura microcosmus	Pyura tessellata	Pyura squamulosa	Microcosmus claudicans
BODY SHAPE	Elongated oval	Flattened	Round or oval	Round or oval
SIPHON SIZE	Large	Very small	Small in diameter and relatively tall	Large in relation to the body size; stripes readily visible on exterior
SIPHON POSITION	Oral siphon at top of body, atrial some way away on side, at an angle	Far apart, on each end of the body	Both siphons on top of body, relatively close together	Both on top of body
BODY TEXTURE	Rough and lumpy often covered in debris	Warty, with concentric lines and/or hexagonal plates all over	Smoother than the other 3 with rounded plates of concentric lines all over	Rough / tessellated, often covered with debris with only siphons showing
SIPHON COLOUR	Cream and orange, often with rose-red stripes	Purple with bright pink edge, but not striped	Violet stripes alternating with white	Noticeably bright colours of white / lilac / orange
SIZE	10cm	1cm	2.5cm	4cm
DISTRIBUTION	Scattered	Scattered	Scattered	Scattered
ABUNDANCE	Occasional	Occasional	Occasional	Rare
DEPTH				
HABITAT				

Pyura microcosmus (Savigny, 1816)

Pyura microcosmus. Loch Creran, Argyll and Bute.

A unitary sea squirt with a leathery test, often completely covered in detritus so that only the siphons are visible. Where the body can be seen, it is dirty brown, orange or red in colour, with scattered wart-like lumps. The siphons are reasonably long but very sensitive to disturbance, and retract rapidly, becoming square in shape. When fully expanded, they have distinctive internal longitudinal double stripes of orange, white and sometimes pink-red. The stripe pattern is extremely variable, ranging from the palest caramel and white to vivid red, orange and white. The red is often restricted to deep inside the siphons. Animals found in Scottish sea lochs seem to be markedly larger and more brightly coloured than those found elsewhere. It is found in sheltered conditions, often attached to shells and rocks.

KEY FEATURES
- Often covered in detritus with only the siphons visible.
- Siphons large and widely spaced, with the atrial siphon at an angle.
- Distinctive orange and white stripes within the siphons, with varying amounts of red.

See also page 87.

Pyura microcosmus. Loch Creran, Argyll and Bute.

Variation in colour of *Pyura microcosmus* siphons

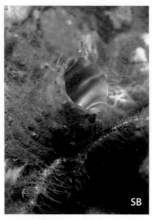

Pyura microcosmus. Pembrokeshire.

Pyura microcosmus. Loch Creran, Argyll and Bute.

Pyura microcosmus. Loch Creran, Argyll and Bute.

An aggregation of *Pyura microcosmus* (caramel and white siphons) with a single *Microcosmus claudicans* (left of centre). Lyme Bay, Devon/Dorset.

Pyura squamulosa (Alder, 1863)

Pyura squamulosa. Small Isles, Highland.

Pyura squamulosa. Isle of Man.

The body is a fat oval or round shape, often with a violet tinge. It is small in size but slightly larger than *P. tessellata*. The test has rounded plates and a smoother appearance than other *Pyura* species. The animal sits upright attached by a broad base with the siphons some distance apart. The pattern on the siphons is of violet to purple stripes, alternating with white.

KEY FEATURES

• Oval rather than flattened body, having a brown or purplish colour overall.
• Large siphons with violet stripes.

See also page 87.

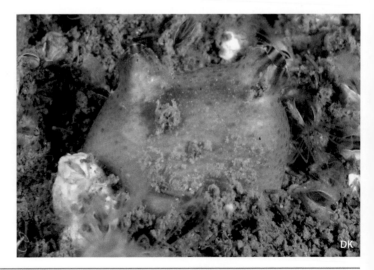

Pyura squamulosa.
Pembrokeshire.

Pyura tessellata

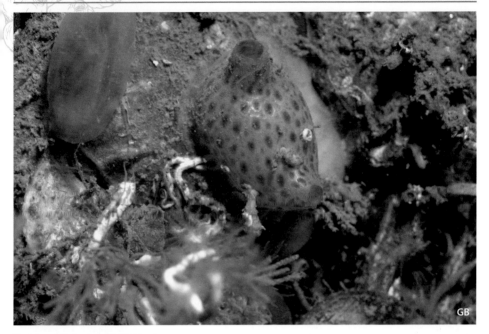

Pyura tessellata. Loch Duich, Highland.

Body usually flattened, brown in colour and attached by an expanded base. The test is leathery in texture and divided into hexagonal or rectangular plates with concentric lines, giving the body a conspicuously tessellated appearance. The siphons are small, pale purple, sometimes edged in red but not striped. They are located at opposite ends of the flattened body.

KEY FEATURES
- Flattened body with tessellated test.
- Small purple siphons at each end.

See also page 87.

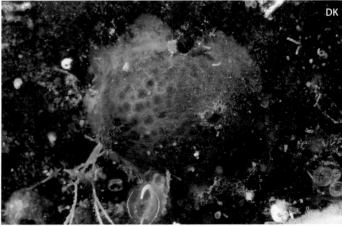

Pyura tessellata with small, non-striped siphons. Loch Hourn, Highland.

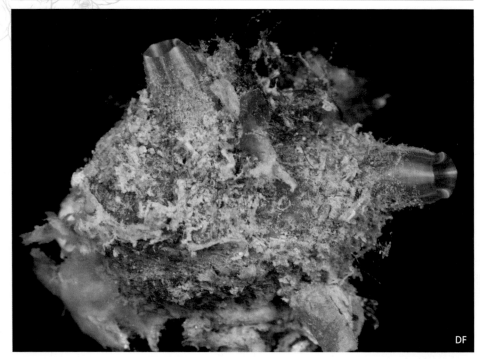

Microcosmus claudicans (not *in situ*). Newlyn, Cornwall.

M. claudicans has a leathery test, and is often completely covered in detritus so that only the siphons are visible. The globular body is wrinkled, red or deep pink in colour and has fine hairs to which sand and detritus adhere. The siphons are large, four-lobed and have a distinctive red or purple, light orange and yellow striped coloration, which can also be seen on the outside. Even where the body is completely obscured, the siphons are readily visible.

KEY FEATURES

- Rounded red body with large siphons.
- Distinctive red and light orange stripes within the siphons visible even when partially contracted.

See also page 87.

Siphons of *Microcosmus claudicans.*
Lyme Bay, Devon/Dorset.

Asterocarpa humilis Compass Sea Squirt (Heller, 1878)

Compass-like siphons of almost completely hidden *Asterocarpa humilis*. Milford Haven, Pembrokeshire.

An orange-red unitary sea squirt, squat in shape and having very flared siphons. There are numerous small warts over the surface, although in the field it is unlikely that these will be seen because this species favours growing in tightly-packed animal turf. The most distinctive feature is the pattern on the inside of the siphons, which alternates four thick with four thinner stripes, like the markings of a compass. A non-native species, it favours harbours and marinas.

KEY FEATURES
- Orange-red and squat in shape.
- Distinctive compass-like pattern of cream and white inside the siphons.

SIMILAR TO The habitat preference and distinctive appearance make this species unlikely to be mis-identified.

DISTRIBUTION:
Scattered: a non-native species first recorded in Britain and Ireland in 2009, it has a patchy distribution along the south coast as far west as Newlyn as well as records from Oban marina, Holyhead, Milford Haven, and Strangford Lough.

ABUNDANCE:
Occasional

Botrylloides spp.

These compound species form thin, encrusting sheets. Their zooids are arranged to varying degrees in parallel rows, separated by water channels that can give the appearance of an encrusting sponge. They are variously predated upon by *Trivia*, nudibranchs such as *Goniodoris castanea*, and the flatworm *Cycloporus papillosus* (see pages 112–115).

A number of species are found in British and Irish waters, including several that are non-native, but identification to species level can be difficult except in certain situations. *B. leachii* is a native species often found on seaweed and rocky surfaces exposed to water movement, generally in relatively shallow water. A colour morph with a distinct 'cartwheel' pattern of colour around the inhalant openings was originally described as *B. radiata* by Alder and Hancock (1848), but is now synonymised with *B. leachii*. *B. violaceus* is a non-native species, originally from Japan and first recorded in Britain and Ireland in 2004. It is generally found in harbours and marinas, and intertidally on seaweed in sheltered locations. In some locations on the south coast of England another non-native (*B. diegensis*) is also found. Additional morphologically distinct forms (including a speckled variant currently termed *Botrylloides* sp. X) are regularly observed by divers; photographic records would be of interest (see photo on page 102).

KEY FEATURES

- Thin sheets with zooids arranged in a mixture of oval groups and parallel lines that meander and occasionally branch, depending on the species.
- *B. leachii* is usually bright orange, yellow or pink in colour, although patterned forms can also be found. One variant (*radiata*) has a distinct 'cartwheel' pattern of colour around the inhalant openings.
- *B. violaceus* is always a single colour (bright orange, violet, brick red, pink or yellow) and has very big red-pink larvae brooded in the matrix of the colony.
- *B. diegensis* has white, yellow or orange zooids that contrast markedly with a darker test, or can be a single colour. In the contrasting colour scheme, individual zooids show fairly consistent teardrop-shaped pigmentation. Zooids appear to be arranged in less of a distinct pattern than for other *Botrylloides* species, meandering in loops or short rows.

SIMILAR TO *Botryllus schlosseri* can be distinguished from *Botrylloides* species by having zooids that are arranged in a star-like pattern as opposed to parallel rows. *Aplidium nordmanni* and *Aplidium elegans* can look superficially similar to a *Botrylloides* species, but they form raised masses as opposed to thin sheets. *Botrylloides* can also be mistaken for encrusting sponges due to their water channels and oscule-like cloacal openings.

Unicolour specimens of *B. violaceus*, *B. diegensis* and *B. leachii* can be difficult to separate in the field. *B. leachii* seems to have the zooids predominantly arranged in relatively long, zipper-like parallel-sided double rows. In contrast, *B. violaceus* zooids are typically arranged in much shorter double rows that branch and can form small circles. A definitive identification of *B. violaceus* can be made by inspecting the larvae, which during the summer reproductive season can be seen being brooded in the matrix of the colony. *B. violaceus* is unique in having very large larvae, approximately the size of an individual zooid and red-pink whatever the colony colour, and with 25–30 readily visible ampullae. In contrast, *B. leachii* and *B. diegensis* larvae are much smaller and have only 8 ampullae.

Given the difficulties in field identification, it is recommended that observations are recorded as '*Botrylloides* sp.' except in the following situations:

- A specimen with strikingly coloured zooids (often with a teardrop shape to the pigmentation and a raised rim around each inhalant opening) against a dark test is *B. diegensis*.
- A specimen with a characteristic pattern of secondary markings around each inhalant opening is *B. leachii* var. *radiata*.
- A unicolour specimen with very large pink-red larvae is *B. violaceus*.

Botrylloides leachii (Savigny, 1816)

Paired zooid arrangement of *Botrylloides leachii*. Dorset.

Botrylloides leachii. Farne Islands, Northumberland.

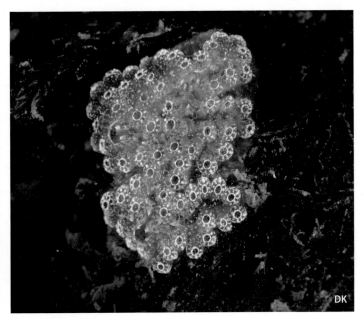

'Cartwheel' markings around the oral openings of *Botrylloides leachii* var. *radiata*. Farne Islands, Northumberland.

DISTRIBUTION:
Widespread: all around Britain and Ireland

ABUNDANCE:
Frequent

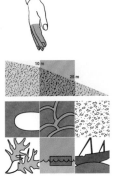

Botrylloides violaceus Orange Cloak Sea Squirt Oka, 1927

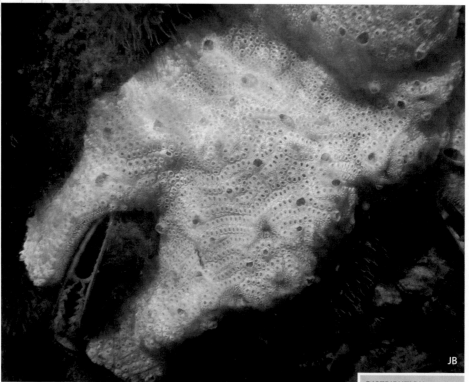

Uniform yellow *Botrylloides violaceus*. Plymouth, Devon.

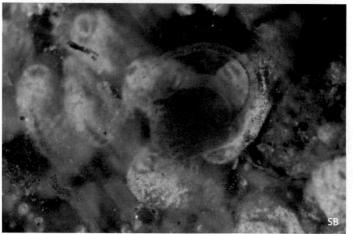

Red larvae of *Botrylloides violaceus* with visible ampullae, amongst orange zooids. Milford Haven, Pembrokeshire.

DISTRIBUTION:
Scattered: generally found on the south coast of England, but has also been recorded in Milford Haven and Ireland.

ABUNDANCE:
Occasional

Botrylloides diegensis San Diego Sea Squirt Ritter & Forsyth, 1917

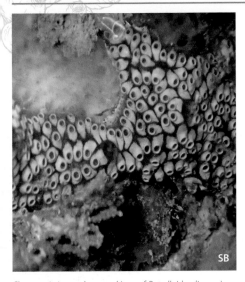

Characteristic teardrop markings of *Botrylloides diegensis*. Portland Marina, Dorset.

Cream variant of *Botrylloides diegensis*. Poole Bay, Dorset.

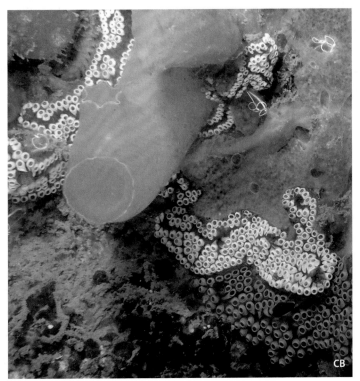

Two colour variants of *Botrylloides diegensis* in mixed sea squirt turf. Portland Marina, Dorset.

DISTRIBUTION:
Restricted or localised distribution: south coast of England

ABUNDANCE:
Occasional

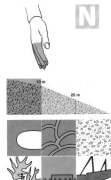

SD

Botryllus schlosseri growing around the base of a kelp stipe. Sark, Channel Islands.

Botryllus schlosseri Star Sea Squirt

(Pallas, 1766)

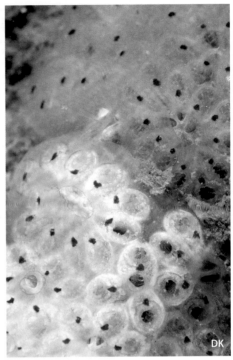

Botryllus schlosseri. Pembrokeshire.

Botryllus schlosseri. Pembrokeshire.

A common species that forms encrusting sheets with distinctive star-like systems of zooids arranged around a common cloacal opening. This species is highly variable in colour, with the star-like arrangement particularly visible in specimens with contrasting coloration. Found in a range of habitats from the lower shore, seaweed and kelp stipes in shallow water, and exposed rock surfaces, it is commonest in locations with considerable current or wave action.

Although highly variable in colour, colonies appear to group into one of two morphological forms. One form consists of opaque colonies, often with contrasting colours and a classic star-like appearance. The second has colonies that are semi-transparent and uniformly white, blue or yellow, without the contrasting pigmentation. A dark red spot is readily visible in the middle of each zooid in this second group, and the colonies appear to form thicker sheets, especially when wrapped around kelp stipes. At the present time both forms should be recorded as *Botryllus schlosseri*.

DISTRIBUTION:
Widespread

ABUNDANCE:
Abundant

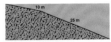

KEY FEATURES
- Encrusting sheet with a star-like arrangement of zooids.
- May have a single darker spot near the middle of each zooid.
- Highly variable in coloration.

SIMILAR TO *Botrylloides* species have meandering lines of paired zooids rather than the distinctive star-like zooid arrangement. Smaller pink specimens may also resemble *Aplidium nordmanni* or *Aplidium elegans*, but the zooid arrangement is different and these two other species form rounded lumps as opposed to an encrusting sheet.

Colours of *Botryllus schlosseri*

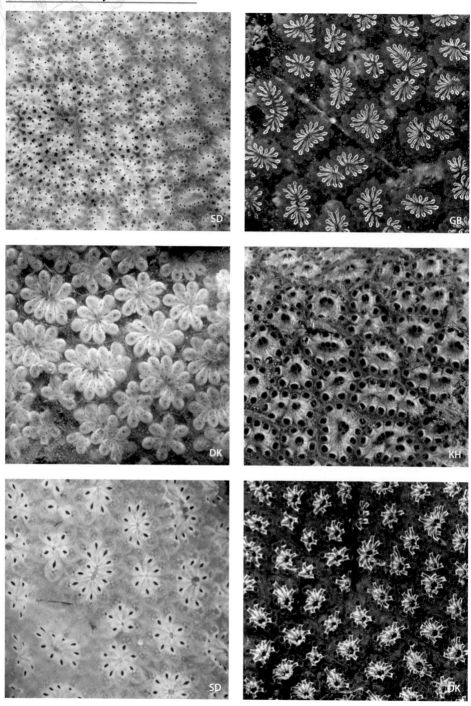

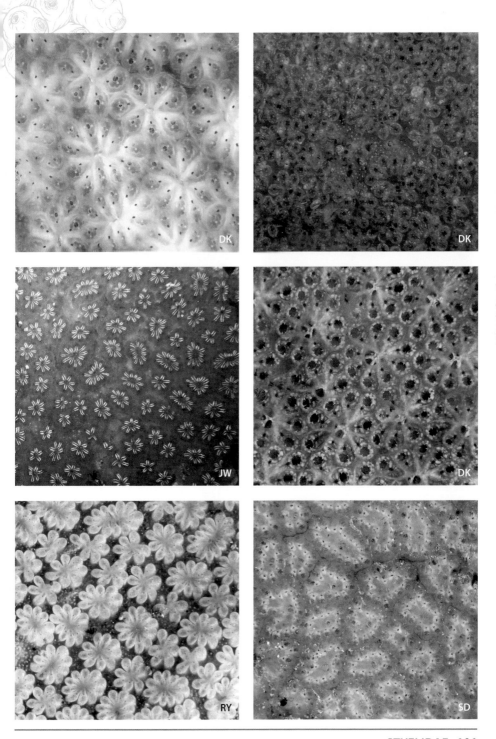

Zooid arrangement in botryllid sea squirts

Although *Botryllus* and *Botrylloides* colonies can appear similar, their zooids are in fact arranged in fundamentally different ways. Understanding this difference is useful so as to avoid confusion between species. For example, *Botrylloides* specimens that show circles of zooids might be misinterpreted as the star-like systems of *B. schlosseri*.

The zooids of both *Botryllus* and *Botrylloides* colonies are arranged into systems (defined as a group of zooids that share the same common cloacal opening). In *Botryllus*, these systems are very localised, with a small number of zooids arranged in a circle around a single central cloacal opening. Each system is then separated from the next by cellulose tunic, resulting in the star-like pattern of *B. schlosseri*.

Botryllus schlosseri systems showing circles of zooids with a central common cloacal opening.

However, in the case of *Botrylloides* the zooids first expel water into channels that form a maze through the colony. These water channels have periodic cloacal openings from which water is finally released into the sea. As a consequence, individual zooids may be some distance from the cloacal opening, being connected to it by the intervening water channel.

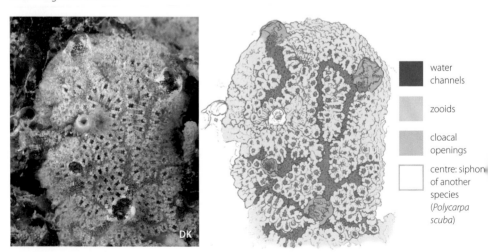

water channels

zooids

cloacal openings

centre: siphon of another species (*Polycarpa scuba*)

Botrylloides sp. X showing zooids connected to cloacal openings via water channels.

This leads to overall differences in zooid arrangement in *Botryllus* and *Botrylloides* colonies. For example, the use of water channels means that there is a more-or-less continuous line of zooids at the margin of a *Botrylloides* colony, whereas in *B. schlosseri* a series of separate ovals of zooids occupy the colony edge. This is one feature that can help distinguish between *Botryllus* and *Botrylloides* colonies.

Confusingly, *Botrylloides* colonies can sometimes show what appear to be circular groupings of zooids that might be mistaken for *B. schlosseri* systems. However, these circles of zooids in *Botrylloides* do not have a cloacal opening in the centre of the group, with zooids instead discharging water into a water channel that surrounds the circle. These 'pseudosystems' can be particularly prominent in some *Botrylloides* specimens.

Presumed *B. violaceus* colony on a panel, closed up so that the arrangement of zooids is very plain, with numerous superficially *Botryllus*-like 'systems'.

Dendrodoa grossularia (Van Beneden, 1846)

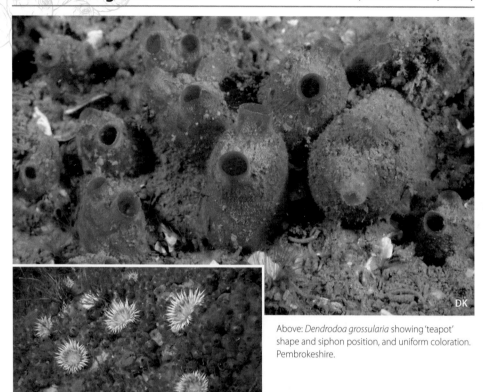

DK

Above: *Dendrodoa grossularia* showing 'teapot' shape and siphon position, and uniform coloration. Pembrokeshire.

Left: a dense aggregation of *Dendrodoa grossularia* interspersed with *Sagartia elegans* anemones. Isle of Man.

CW

A unitary sea squirt that is squat in shape, with round, unmarked siphons projecting from the upper side of the body. Individuals are red, reddish-orange or reddish-brown in colour, generally smooth and can appear discoloured or dirty-looking. Found in a wide range of habitats, from very exposed shallow surge gullies to rocky reefs in sheltered conditions. In areas of strong water movement individuals tend to be flatter, more dome-shaped, and well-separated from each other. In more sheltered conditions they grow taller, with local settlement of larvae often leading to dense aggregations of closely-packed but separate individuals.

KEY FEATURES
- Small and squat 'teapot' shape, solid red in colour with small round siphons.
- Often found in dense aggregations, usually relatively clean.

SIMILAR TO *Stolonica socialis* has a more upright ('coffee pot') shape and is orange in colour. *Distomus variolosus* is smaller, with individual zooids partially submerged in the basal test, and often found with two-tone coloration. *Polycarpa scuba* is larger, a mix of white and red, and has longer siphons that flare out at the end. *Polycarpa errans* (not described here) is similarly unicolour but has longer, flared siphons. *Styela coriacea* (not described here) has a similar depressed appearance to the version of *D. grossularia* found in exposed conditions, but has a wrinked test covered with small tubercles and a far more expanded base (see photo page 105).

DISTRIBUTION:
Widespread

ABUNDANCE:
Abundant

Dendrodoa grossularia interspersed with the sponge *Clathrina coriacea*, which defines the habitat 'infralittoral rock in a surge gully'. Isle of Man.

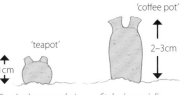

'coffee pot'

'teapot'

1cm

2–3cm

Dendrodoa grossularia   *Stolonica socialis*

Diagrammatic representation of the different shape/size of individuals in these two species.

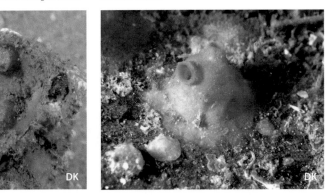

Individual *Dendrodoa grossularia* on a bivalve shell. Note the flatter shape. Pembrokeshire.

Spreading test of *Styela coriacea*. Strangford Lough, Co. Down.

Distomus variolosus
Gaertner, 1774

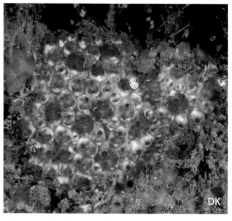

Above: Prominent two-tone 'rhubarb and custard' colourway may be *D. hupferi* (not described here). Pembrokeshire.

Left: *Distomus variolosus* growing around a kelp stipe. Lizard, Cornwall.

This sea squirt forms colonies of densely packed small rounded zooids, partially submerged in a common basal test. Each zooid has a pair of small siphons, often showing six faint stripes. Overall, colonies are dark red to brownish, shiny, and the zooids often have a faintly two-tone colour. Most commonly found on kelp holdfasts, it can also be found on rock. (Specimens with a pronounced 'rhubarb and custard' coloration are likely *D. hupferi*, not described here.)

KEY FEATURES
- Colonies composed of small densely packed round zooids, fused together part way down the side.
- Shiny red, sometimes two-tone in colour.

SIMILAR TO *Dendrodoa grossularia* (often found in the same habitat, intermixed with *Distomus*) can also form dense aggregations, but the individual animals are larger than the zooids of *Distomus*, and are not partially embedded in a common basal test.

DISTRIBUTION:
Scattered: Primarily a south and western species that is quite common in south-west Wales and the south coast of England as far east as Dorset. Although there have been occasional records from Scotland, it seems likely that these are a mis-recording of *Dendrodoa grossularia*

ABUNDANCE:
Frequent

Zooids forming large colonies.

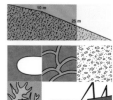

Distomus variolosus growing over a rocky reef. Pembrokeshire.

Polycarpa fibrosa

(Stimpson, 1852)

Polycarpa fibrosa (red and yellow siphons) amongst the white siphons of *P. scuba*. Pembrokeshire.

A small unitary sea squirt typically found partially buried in gravel or sediment, usually with only the siphons visible. The siphons are long and delicate, marked with red. If visible, the test is covered with fibrils that trap sand particles, so that it is completely encrusted apart from the siphons and an area around them. It appears to favour moderately exposed sites with tidal streams.

KEY FEATURES
- Long, delicate siphons marked with red.
- Smooth siphon rims.
- Buried in gravel or sediment.

SIMILAR TO Several molgulids are found buried in sediment but have small crown-like projections on the rim of their oral siphons, whereas *P. fibrosa* has smooth siphon rims.

DISTRIBUTION:
Scattered: found all round Britain and Ireland but uncommon. May be frequent in suitable locations. Most records are from offshore dredge samples in the North Sea.

ABUNDANCE:
Occasional

Polycarpa fibrosa siphons. Pembrokeshire.

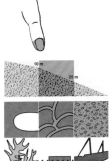

Polycarpa pomaria

(Savigny, 1816)

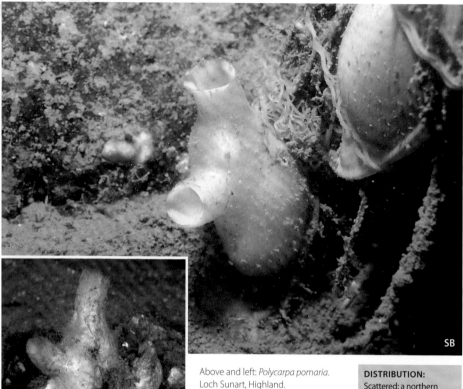

SB

Above and left: *Polycarpa pomaria*.
Loch Sunart, Highland.

DK

DISTRIBUTION:
Scattered: a northern species quite common in western Scotland. Records from further south than the Irish Sea may be a different species.

ABUNDANCE:
Frequent

A pale, unitary sea squirt that tends to be found in prominent positions on reefs, attached to rocks and shells. Ranging from off-white through grey to brown, it usually appears somewhat dirty. The body is conical, broadest at its base where it attaches to the rock. The test is thick and leathery and has a bumpy surface. The siphons are long and slightly fluted, with the oral siphon at the top and curved to one side, and the atrial siphon off at an angle. It has a distinctive very fine red stripe outlining the rims of both siphons, usually more obvious on the oral siphon. Some animals show markings inside the siphons ranging from faint white lines to pinky orange stripes. Favours sheltered and semi-sheltered conditions.

KEY FEATURES
- A large pale-coloured species with a wrinkled, leathery test.
- Conical in shape with long siphons terminating in a fine red stripe.

SIMILAR TO *P. scuba* is smaller, has a thinner test and coloration that ranges from pink to darker red, with siphons always paler than the body. Larger specimens of *Pyura microcosmus* may also appear similar but have siphons that are more obviously striped, longer and less fluted than those of *P. pomaria*.

Polycarpa scuba Monniot, 1971

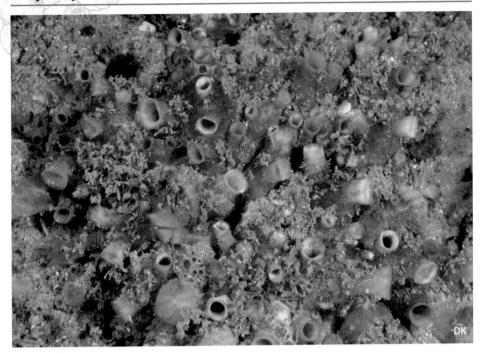

Polycarpa scuba. Pembrokeshire.

A unitary sea squirt that often has some detritus attached to it, giving a dirty appearance. It is red or pinkish in colour with paler siphons that are large in relation to the body size. The siphons flare out considerably when fully expanded and look square when partially closed. It tolerates a variety of locations, from strong water movement to sheltered areas. Can be found singly but also seen in large numbers alongside other similar squirts.

DISTRIBUTION:
Widespread: commoner in the west and on the south coast.

ABUNDANCE:
Frequent

KEY FEATURES
- Rounded body, red or pinkish in colour.
- Paler flared siphons.

SIMILAR TO *Dendrodoa grossularia* can look very similar to *P. scuba* and is also found in many of the same locations. However, *D. grossularia* has smaller siphons which are never paler than the body. *P. errans* (*P. rustica* in some texts) is similar but uniform in colour, and lacks the contrasting paler siphons (not described here, see picture right).

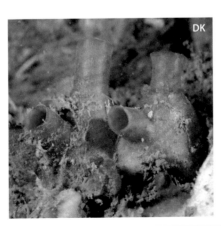

Polycarpa errans. Pembrokeshire.

Stolonica socialis

Hartmeyer, 1903

Stolonica socialis with the anemone *Actinothoe sphyrodeta*. Devon.

This is a stoloniferous species, with individual zooids arising singly from a basal stolon that is hidden from view. Individuals are pale yellow-orange to bright orange in colour with a thin, semi-transparent test. Siphons are round in shape, located at the top of the body, and diverge slightly. Individuals are noticeably taller than they are wide. Stoloniferous growth results in dense aggregations, although it should be noted that non-stoloniferous species such as *Dendrodoa grossularia* can also form dense aggregations. *S. socialis* prefers deeper clear water and exposure to reasonable water movement, and may be locally common in sand-scoured habitats, with large colonies attached to bedrock, boulders or occasionally even gravel.

DISTRIBUTION:
Widespread with a bias: predominantly a south and western species which occurs as far as north-west Ireland but not round the west of Scotland.

ABUNDANCE:
Frequent

KEY FEATURES

- Clean test that is yellow-orange or bright orange, never red.
- Individuals are taller than they are wide ('coffee pot' as opposed to 'teapot' in proportions, see page 105).

SIMILAR TO *Dendrodoa grossularia* has a more rounded 'teapot' shape, and is a red to red-orange in colour, rather than the yellow-orange colour of *S. socialis*. *Polycarpa scuba* can appear similar to *S. socialis* but has larger flared siphons that are paler than the body.

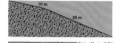

Styela clava Leathery Sea Squirt

Herdman, 1881

Above: *Styela clava* attached to a pebble by a narrow stalk. Poole Bay, Dorset.

Left: brown striped siphons and warty appearance of *Styela clava*. Plymouth, Devon.

DISTRIBUTION:
Widespread with a bias: this non-native species was first recorded in Plymouth in 1953. It is presumed to have been introduced on the hulls of warships returning from the Korean War. It is now fairly widespread around south and south-east coasts, Wales, Western Scotland, Larne Lough, and Mulroy Bay in Ireland but no records from east coasts north of the Humber Estuary.

ABUNDANCE:
Abundant

A very distinctive unitary sea squirt that is unique amongst British and Irish species in having a long narrow body tapering to an obvious stalk. The surface of the dirty brown body is tough and leathery, with folds and swellings that give it a warty appearance. However, it is often so heavily encrusted with other organisms that it is difficult to see the overall shape. Both siphons are situated close together at the top end, and have brownish-purple and cream stripes. Generally found singly, attached to solid surfaces in shallow water, especially in harbours and marinas, but in suitable locations can also be found on wrecks and natural rock substrates.

KEY FEATURES
- Slim leathery body that tapers down to a tough stalk.
- Often heavily encrusted.
- Siphons are located close together at the free end of the animal and have four brown stripes on the inside.

SIMILAR TO Unlikely to be mistaken for any other British or Irish sea squirt.

Sea squirt predators

Despite their tough cellulose tunic, some predators have specialised feeding apparatuses that enable them to gain access to the soft internal organs of sea squirts. The two main groups of sea squirt predators are molluscs and flatworms.

Molluscs that prey on sea squirts include the nudibranchs *Goniodoris castanea* (which feeds on botryllids), *G. nodosa*, *Okenia aspersa*, and *O. elegans* (all of which eat unitary sea squirts). Others include the tiny sea slug *Colpodaspis pusilla* (which eats small sea squirts such as *Pycnoclavella*) and the much larger *Pleurobranchus membranaceus*. Other sea squirt consuming molluscs include the cowries, *Trivia arctica* and *T. monacha*; the Velvet Snail *Velutina velutina*; and *Lamellaria perspicua* and *L. latens*, all of which also embed their egg capsules in the test of their prey. *L. latens* often has small black or sepia flecks that mimic the small inhalant pores on compound sea squirts such as *Trididemnum*, thus camouflaging it while on its prey.

Sea squirt predators amongst the flatworms include *Cycloporus papillosus*, which feeds on botryllids, and the Candy Striped Flatworm *Prostheceraeus vittatus*, which eats the Lightbulb Sea Squirt *Clavelina lepadiformis*.

Flatworms

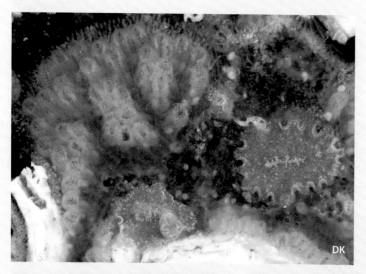

Left: *Cycloporus papillosus* with *Botrylloides* sp. Isle of Man.

Bottom left: *Prostheceraeus vittatus* with *Clavelina lepadiformis*. Dartmouth, Devon.

Bottom right: *Prostheceraeus vittatus* on *Diazona violacea*. Loch Hourn, Highland.

Nudibranchs

Left: *Okenia elegans.* Pembrokeshire.

Below left: *Okenia elegans*, partially inside a unitary sea squirt with only its gills visible. Brixham, Devon.

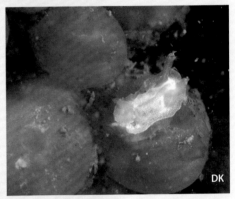

Above right: *Goniodoris nodosa* on *Dendrodoa grossularia*. Pembrokeshire.

Left: *Goniodoris castanea.* Loch Eil, Highland.

Other molluscs

The cowrie *Trivia arctica* pictured on *Stolonica socialis*. Pembrokeshire.

The tiny sea slug *Colpodaspis pusilla*, which has an internal shell, next to *Clavelina lepadiformis*. It has also been reported to feed on *Pycnoclavella stolonialis*. Jura, Argyll and Bute.

Lamellaria perspicua on a compound sea squirt. Norfolk.

Lamellaria latens (right, small) and *L. perspicua* (left) showing markings similar to that of a didemnid sea squirt. Farne Islands, Northumberland.

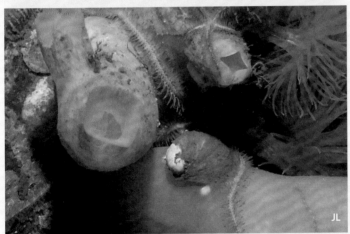

The gastropod mollusc *Velutina velutina*, plus egg capsules laid in the test of *Ascidia virginea*. Loch Fyne, Argyll and Bute.

Multiple egg capsules of the Velvet Snail *Velutina velutina* embedded in the test of an *Ascidia* sp. Loch Creran, Argyll and Bute.

INTRODUCTION TO SPONGES

This limestone wall in Dorset is almost entirely covered in encrusting sponges.

Diverse branching and massive sponges with large colonies of the bryozoan *Pentapora foliacea*. Isles of Scilly, Cornwall.

Phylum Porifera

Sponges are very simple sessile, aquatic animals. Sponges are not colonies – each sponge can be regarded as an individual animal. However, they lack characteristics found in other multi-cellular animals, such as nerve and muscle cells and sensory organs. They are also capable of cell dissociation and re-aggregation – some species can re-form into an individual even after their cells are separated by straining through a muslin cloth. Sponge tissue contains more than 12 different cell types with various functions such as skeleton secretion. Special cells called archaeocytes are also present – these are like stem cells and can produce any other sponge cell type.

The scientific name for the group means pore-bearing and is derived from the fact that the surface of a sponge has a large number of holes in it. These are part of the aquiferous system, a network of pores, canals and chambers perforating their body, which allows the sponges to obtain food and oxygen from the water. Water is drawn into the sponge by a current created by the beating of tiny whip-like cells called choanocytes. It enters through small pores called ostia, and is fed into the choanocyte chambers via incurrent canals. It exits via exhalant canals though larger holes called oscules. These are often situated on extremities so that water does not go through the system twice. Ostia are often too small to see, but oscules are usually visible

A choanocyte chamber from a species of *Oscarella*. The choanocytes are arranged around the edge of the circular chamber with their flagellae directed inwards.

and their arrangement can be a useful identification characteristic. Some species also have characteristic patterns of canals which may be visible as star or mesh patterns through a translucent outer layer.

In some small sponges, the aquiferous system has a very simple tubular (asconoid) organisation. Others have a slightly more complicated arrangement where the lining of the tube is folded to create several chambers (syconoid). In most demosponges, the aquiferous system is quite a complicated network of circular chambers joined by connecting channels (leuconoid). These types of aquiferous systems are thought to have evolved several times, and therefore a simpler organisation does not mean that a sponge species is necessarily more primitive. In some sponges, the aquiferous system has been lost completely (see section on feeding pages 120–121).

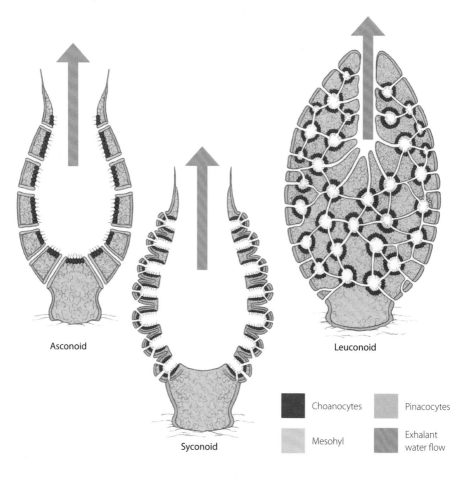

Asconoid

Syconoid

Leuconoid

Choanocytes   Pinacocytes

Mesohyl   Exhalant water flow

The arrangement of cells, chambers and channels in the three main types of aquiferous system.

Sponge classification

There are four main living groups (classes) of sponges and one exclusively fossil class:

Class Calcarea – calcium carbonate spicules, marine only. Usually white or grey in colour and fairly small. This group requires considerable taxonomic work, and many taxa currently regarded as species may in fact be complexes of several species. Twenty-nine valid species are currently recognised from Britain and Ireland.

Class Demospongiae – name means 'the common sponges', about 85% of living sponges belong in this class and it contains the only freshwater species. Demosponges usually have silica spicules, but these can be supplemented or replaced by a skeleton of flexible spongin fibres. This class contains sponges of a huge variety of colours and forms. There are currently 344 species recognised as valid from Britain and Ireland.

Class Homoscleromorpha – silica skeleton, where present. Recently separated from demosponges on the basis of DNA studies. The genus *Oscarella*, belongs to this class. Four species are recognised from Britain and Ireland.

Class Hexactinellidae – silica skeleton including six-rayed spicules. Exclusively marine but mainly occur in deep water so not included in this guide. Usually white or grey in colour. Come in a wide variety of forms.

Class Archaeocyatha – exclusively fossil sponges, no known living examples.

Many sponges have a spongin fibre skeleton, and the majority have smaller skeletal elements called spicules which are formed from silica (in Demospongiae, Hexactinellidae and Homoscleromorpha) and calcium carbonate (in Calcarea). Sponges are classified based on the arrangement of their skeletal fibres and the size and shape of their spicules which come in a vast array of forms. The skeleton is only visible under a microscope, and specialist techniques are needed to prepare slides to view specimens. However, by examining the skeleton and comparing this to *in situ* appearance, sponge researchers have built up a good knowledge of the external form of many British and Irish species.

Ideally the form, dimensions, surface detail and colour of the live sponge should be recorded by photography. This enables identification to be confirmed at a later date if necessary. There are some rare species where Seasearch records would be particularly welcome – we have indicated these in the text. However, in general all sponges are under-recorded, and records will greatly help in understanding the distribution and ecology of this important phylum.

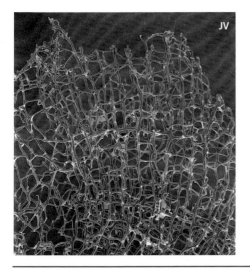

The spongin fibre skeleton of *Spongionella pulchella* as seen under scanning electron microscope when the surrounding tissue has been dissolved away.

Reproduction

Both asexual and sexual reproduction occurs in sponges. Asexual reproduction ranges from regeneration from sponge fragments to more complex processes such as the formation of buds and gemmules (tough spore-like structures that can survive difficult conditions). Sexual reproduction also occurs – most sponges are successively hermaphrodite and change from male to female, producing eggs and sperm at different times.

Small buds developing on the golf ball sponge *Tethya citrina*. These will eventually fall off the parent sponge and become new individuals.

The majority of sponges are viviparous. Fertilisation of eggs and larval development take place within the sponge. Sperm are released from and enter the sponge via its aquiferous system. Short-lived larvae are then released via the aquiferous system, and these change into adult sponges after they have settled on a suitable substrate. However, there are several variations: for example some species produce crawling larvae and some incubate young sponges. Some species are oviparous, where eggs can be fertilised internally before they are released, or gametes may be released and fertilised in the water. The embryos develop outside the parent sponge, either via a swimming larval stage or directly.

Feeding

Most sponges feed by filtering particles from the water which flows through them. Larger particles (0.5–50µm) are trapped in the ostia (water entry pores), but bacteria sized particles <0.5µm (typically 80% of a sponge's food supply) are captured by the choanocytes. Many species host photosynthesising organisms between their cells in a symbiotic (mutually beneficial) relationship. Symbiotic bacteria can form a third of the mass of living tissue in some species. Some sponges may gain up to 80% of their energy supply from symbiotic organisms.

In some demosponge families including the Cladorhizidae, which largely occur in the deep sea where suspended food is in short supply, the aquiferous system has been lost completely and feeding is carnivorous. These sponges use hook-like small spicules, thread-like structures, or even balloon-like structures to capture prey such as small shrimps which are then engulfed. Although not currently known from Britain and Ireland, a species of carnivorous sponge, *Lycopodina hypogea* has recently been recorded from shallow water (5–50m) in several areas including Brittany, and could therefore reasonably be expected to occur in southern Britain.

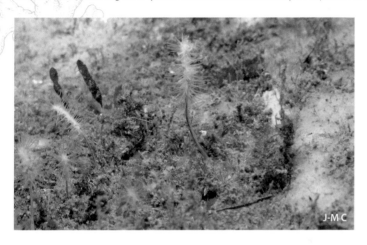

The carnivorous sponge *Lycopodina hypogea*, Ile de Groix, Brittany.

Predation

Many species of sponges have chemical compounds in their tissues which can protect them against threats such as predation, pathogens and biofouling. Some of these are being developed by the pharmaceutical industry as they have medicinal properties – for example compounds from the common shore sponge *Hymeniacidon perlevis* have been shown to inhibit growth of breast and lung cancer cells. Despite their defensive compounds, many animals are able to eat sponges. These include several species of sea slug which are often perfectly camouflaged against their prey. *Rostanga rubra* feeds on the encrusting sponges *Ophlitaspongia papilla* and *Microciona atrasanguinea*, and *Doris sticta* is often found on yellow sponges such as *Ciocalypta penicillus*.

The sea slug *Doris sticta* and sponge *Ciocalypta penicillus*.

Growth

Sponge growth may be very variable, even within the same species. The ultimate size and form of a sponge is governed by environmental factors such as water motion or predation. Growth rate varies widely between species; some species may go from settlement to larval production in just a few months; others show little growth and individuals may be many decades old. Growth and reproduction in sponges is often seasonal.

Ecological importance

Sponges are often spatially dominant in our benthic marine habitats. As they have both fast and slow growing forms and have a plastic growth form, they can take advantage of a wide variety of conditions. Sponges play an important functional role linking the open water column and benthic dwelling species. They are a key part of the carbon, silicon and nitrogen (due to their symbionts) cycles of marine ecosystems. Sponge growth can help to stabilise mobile substrates such as boulders, and the presence of sponges increases the settlement of larvae of other taxa. Sponges themselves can be an important habitat for other organisms – for example a study of animals living in six Tunisian species found 11 different phyla and 1,500 individuals per kilogram of sponge tissue.

Sponges can aid the settlement of other invertebrates such as these juvenile starfish. Isles of Scilly, Cornwall.

Featherstars living on a Prawn Cracker Sponge *Axinella infundibuliformis*. Pembrokeshire.

Habitat

Most sponges grow on rock, but they may also colonise artificial substrates and some species typically grow on seaweeds or shells. Some species can tolerate silt but many cannot, so sponge communities are often most abundant on vertical or overhanging rock faces. Sponges are most prolific in areas of strong water flow: areas with strong tidal currents or strong wave movement, such as surge gullies. Most species prefer fully saline sea-water although some species can tolerate reduced salinity conditions found in estuaries. There are also freshwater sponges, but these are not covered in this book. We have given approximate depth ranges for species in the text, but these are not exact – sublittoral species can occur intertidally in well-shaded

Sponges can often be found growing on the carapace of spider crabs such as this *Inachus* sp. Anglesey.

crevices and caves. Geographical distribution is not completely known either, as many areas, such as the east coast of England, are poorly sampled. Therefore, whilst we have given a suggestion of distribution in the text, this is not absolute and new Seasearch records, particularly from poorly sampled areas or of rare species, are very useful.

Sponges can be found in the intertidal on the underside of boulders. Kent.

Taxonomy and distribution

Sponges remain a poorly known group: there are currently 8,744 species described in the scientific literature, but scientists estimate that there may be as many as 15,000 species worldwide. A recent study of the sponges of Rathlin Island (a small island off the northern Irish coast) found 28 species new to science (Picton & Goodwin, 2007), demonstrating that there are still many discoveries to be made even in areas with a supposedly well known fauna such as Britain and Ireland. Many sponges have been described from their preserved appearance. As they lose colour and their form becomes distorted when preserved, this gives no indication of their appearance in the field. It is only comparatively recently with the development of underwater photography and the work of scientists on such guides as the Marine Conservation Society Sponge series that we are able to link species names to their living appearance. As their larval phase is short (typical survival estimated as under four days), colonisation of new areas is a slow process and many species have restricted distributions. Recent research also indicates that many species are restricted to particular depth ranges.

Terms used in the descriptions

We have divided the species in the book on the basis of morphology. This has no relation to higher taxonomy, but we felt it was the easiest character to classify sponges for *in situ* identification. Some species have a variety of morphological forms, and in this case they are classified under that which is most typical.

Branching sponges
Branching may be horizontal (branching-repent) or upright (branching-erect). In upright forms, branching can be regular (e.g. dichotomous branching where each branch is continuously sub-divided into two) or irregular.

Cup, vase or fan shaped sponges
Resembling a vase, funnel, cup or fan.

Globular sponges
Ball-shaped sponges; may be a regular sphere or irregular oval. Usually attached by a stalk at their base.

Tubular sponges
Composed of hollow tubes – either a single tube or several joined tubes. We have not included calcareous species which are composed of tubes but have a more obvious overall form here.

Encrusting
Growth laterally over the substrate in the form of thin sheets (<3mm thick) or thicker cushions (3–10mm thick).

Massive
Encrusting sponges which are over 10mm thick and project significantly from the substrate they are attached to. Their surface may be raised in high lobes (lobose) or be almost semi-circular (globose). Species in this category may have fistules or other surface projections but can be distinguished from true branched species as these are on top of a thick basal crust.

Massive with papillae
Some massive sponges have cylindrical or conulose structures known as papillae on their surface.

Examples of different sponge morphologies (forms), from left to right.

Top row: **encrusting** (*Aplysilla rosea*), **massive** (Elephant Hide Sponge *Pachymatisma johnstonia*), **massive with papillae** (Yellow Hedgehog Sponge *Polymastia boletiformis*).

Second row: **globular** (Golf Ball Sponge *Tethya citrina*), **irregular globular** (*Suberites carnosus*), **tubular** (Spiky Lace Sponge *Leucosolenia* sp. with small tubular Purse Sponge *Sycon ciliatum*).

Third row: **stalked vase** (*Haliclona urceolus*), **fan-shaped** (*Phakellia ventilabrum*), **cup-shaped** (Prawn Cracker Sponge *Axinella infundibuliformis*).

Bottom row: **branching-repent** (*Haliclona simulans*), **regular dichotomously branching erect** (*Raspailia hispida*) **irregular branching erect** (Yellow Staghorn Sponge *Axinella dissimilis*).

Terms used describing surface characteristics

Smooth
No projections or depressions.

Conulose
Possessing cone-shaped projections caused by protruding skeletal fibres e.g. Goosebump Sponge *Dysidea fragilis*.

Fistulate
Bearing narrow tubes (fistules), less than 5mm long e.g. *Haliclona fistulosa*.

Papillate
Bearing hollow tubes (papillae) more than 5mm long e.g. Yellow Hedgehog Sponge *Polymastia boletiformis*.

Branching processes
Tassel-like projections from the surface, which may branch e.g. the Shredded Carrot Sponge *Amphilectus fucorum*.

Hispid
Long, closely-packed hairs formed by tufts of spicules e.g. *Stelligera* sp.

Punctate
Surface dotted with pin-point holes e.g. inside of the cup of a Prawn Cracker Sponge *Axinella infundibuliformis*.

Canal patterns
Often visible below the sponge surface, particularly in encrusting species.

Oscules
Large holes through which exhalant water passes.

Ostia
Fine holes through which water enters the sponge – may be hard or impossible to see.

Oscular chimney
Where an oscule is raised on a mound.

Pore sieve
In some species, including the genera *Hymedesmia* and *Phorbas*, the inhalant and exhalant ostia are grouped into circular structures called pore sieves or cribri.

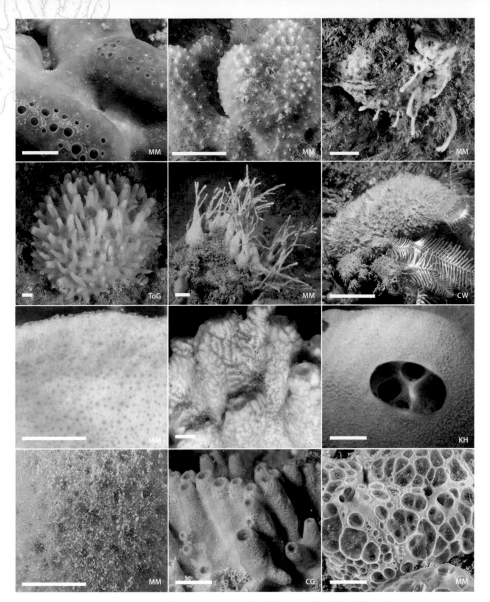

Terms used when describing sponge surface characteristics, all scale bars 1cm, from from left to right.

Top row: **smooth** (Elephant Hide Sponge *Pachymatisma johnstonia*), **conulose** (Goosebump Sponge *Dysidea fragilis*), **fistulate** (*Haliclona fistulosa*).

Second row: **papillate** (Yellow Hedgehog Sponge *Polymastia boletiformis*), **branching processes** (Shredded Carrot Sponge *Amphilectus fucorum*), **hispid** (Purse Sponge *Sycon ciliatum*).

Third row: **punctate** (Prawn Cracker Sponge *Axinella infundibuliformis*), **canal patterns** (*Myxilla incrustans*), **oscule** (Sea Orange *Suberites ficus*).

Bottom row: **ostia** (*Suberites carnosus*), **oscular chimney** (Volcano Sponge *Haliclona viscosa*), **pore sieve** (Crater Sponge *Hemimycale columella*).

How to use this section – sponges

This guide only includes those sponge species found in Britain and Ireland for which *in situ* recognition is possible; this omits many, particularly encrusting, species for which a sample would need to be taken and the spicule skeleton examined under a microscope in order to arrive at a positive identification. That process is beyond the scope of the guide.

As methods of identification develop, species names are updated and do not necessarily match those in the MCS/Ulster Museum Species Directory. The names in use in this guide are the accepted versions at the time of reprinting (2022) according to the World Register of Marine Species (WoRMS).

In the descriptions of individual species, the layout lists the species according to its external shape so species that may be taxonomically distinct are grouped together. Even within the same species the morphology (shape and outward appearance) may vary so we have used the most usual form as a primary key (see page 124).

Branching	pages 130–139
Cup/vase/fan	pages 140–145
Tubular	pages 146–149
Globular	pages 150–153
Thinly encrusting	pages 154–159
Encrusting – spiky	pages 160–163
Massive/thickly encrusting	pages 164–177
Massive or encrusting – with pore sieves	pages 178–183
Massive or encrusting – with projections	pages 185–187
Massive with papillae	pages 189–191

For each species the following information is given, where known:

GENERAL DESCRIPTION

KEY FEATURES The main identifying features for the species.

SIMILAR TO Other sponges with which the species could be confused and how to distinguish them.

DISTRIBUTION the map shows the known distribution in Britain and Ireland taken from Seasearch records, the National Biodiversity Network and other sources. For each area the abundance is shown as:

Common Regularly encountered in suitable habitats in this area.

Occasional Occurs but is not common and distribution may be patchy.

Rare Few records in this area. Observations should be backed up with photographic evidence.

No data No reliable records for this area and any records should be reported and backed up with photographic evidence.

SIZE A guide, using parts of the body, to the size of a typical specimen.

 thumbnail –
less than 1.5cm

 finger tip to thumb joint –
11–15cm

 finger tip to elbow –
30–40cm

 to first thumb joint –
1.5–3cm

 finger tip to wrist –
15–20cm

 finger tip to 3/4 arm length –
40–50cm

 finger length –
3–11cm

 finger tip to mid forearm –
20–30cm

 finger tip to shoulder –
40–60cm

DEPTH Shore includes both the lower shore and rockpools and shallow sublittoral habitats down to about 10m depth, **Mid** depth is from 10m to 25m depth and **Deep** is below 25m.

lower shore and shallow
water 0–10m

mid depth 10–25m

deep water more
than 25m

HABITAT These icons show the habitat(s) in which species can be found.

 Steep vertical bedrock Rocky reef in the form of a wall or pinnacle.

 Gently sloping/ horizontal bedrock Flat(ter) rocky reef.

 Overhangs Rocky reef inclined beyond the vertical, or with deep fissures/caves, providing a shaded environment.

 Boulders and cobbles Rock broken down into smaller units (boulders larger than head-size, down to cobbles which are approximately 6cm and larger).

 Sand and gravel This includes smaller fractions of stone- and biogenic-derived material with particles ranging in size from ~6cm down to fractions of a millimetre.

 Mud Very small particles of stone-derived material smaller than ~60 microns, invisible to the naked eye.

 On other plants or animals Denotes that the species is usually found attached to specific other animals or on seaweeds.

 Wreckage Covers all artificial hard substrates (may be wood, metal etc.).

 Above icons highlighted in orange indicate applicable habitats.

Branching

Axinella dissimilis Yellow Staghorn Sponge (Bowerbank, 1866)

A branched *Axinella dissimilis*. Lyme Bay, Devon/Dorset.

A fan-shaped *Axinella dissimilis*. Sark, Channel Islands.

This bright yellow to orange-yellow branching sponge has a distinctive clean surface with a velvety texture. Its thick (~1.5cm) branches are flattened in cross-section. Typically, several branches arise from near the basal stalk, sometimes these have secondary branching. Often the branches are in one plane, giving an appearance like a candelabra. Sometimes the branches are fused into a fan. The oscules are small and regularly spaced along the branches. Grooves radiate from them in a star pattern, but this may only be apparent out of water.

Found on bedrock on exposed coasts.

Has a south-west distribution in Britain and Ireland; most common in south-west England but occasionally recorded as far north as the west coast of Scotland. This species was previously often reported as *Axinella polypoides*.

KEY FEATURES Branched bright yellow sponge with a velvety surface.

SIMILAR TO May be confused with other branching sponges e.g. *Stelligera montagui* and *Raspailia hispida*, but these typically have thinner branches, are much less bright yellow, and lack the velvety texture of this species.

Haliclona oculata Mermaid's Glove Sponge (Linnaeus, 1759)

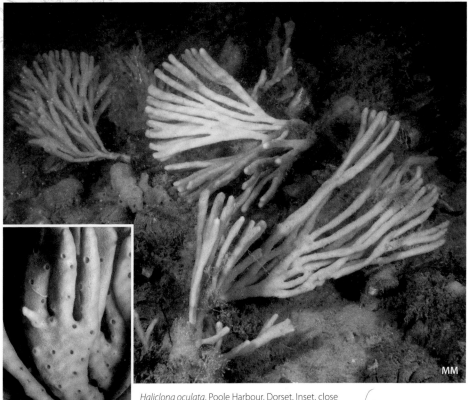

Haliclona oculata. Poole Harbour, Dorset. Inset, close up of oscules of a specimen from Strangford Lough, Co. Down.

A yellow or beige branching sponge with a thin stalk from which arise flattened branches. In some specimens, the branches are simple columns of a fairly uniform thickness; in others they are divided and may widen into paddle-like lobes at their tips. The branches are often different lengths and of irregular thickness, leading to an untidy overall appearance. Specimens may consist of just a single unbranched lobe, but the most spectacular can comprise over 30 branches. The branches bear characteristic small oscules (1–3mm) that are clearly visible, often in lines along the narrow side of the branch. Specimens are often between 10 and 30cm in height but can be larger. The name 'oculata' means with eyes – referring to the rows of eye-like oscules.

Found on rock, wreckage and stones in sediment. Tolerant of silt.

Common on all coasts of Britain and Ireland down to around 100m. May be locally abundant in some areas such as the Menai Strait, North Wales.

KEY FEATURES Yellow or beige sponge with flattened branches displaying distinctive lines of oscules.

SIMILAR TO Could be confused with other yellow branching sponges (e.g. *Axinella dissimilis*, *Raspailia hispida*). However, other branched species lack the distinctive, clearly visible, oscules.

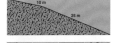

Adreus fascicularis   (Bowerbank, 1866)

Adreus fascicularis in a typical habitat with mobile coarse sand. Swanage Bay, Dorset.

A yellow to brownish-yellow sparsely branched sponge which can be up to 15cm high. The branching is often dichotomous and in one plane, so it can appear antler-like. Branches are circular in cross section and taper to a point. The sponge surface is smooth and oscules are not visible although faint characteristic lines and grooves (striations) can be seen.

Found in sediment over horizontal bedrock and in mobile gravel.

At the northern extent of its range in Britain and Ireland and generally restricted to the English Channel. There are records from Lundy, the Isles of Scilly and North Devon as well as the Channel Islands.

KEY FEATURES Yellow to brownish-yellow sponge having thin, sparse, dichotomous, pointed branches with visible striations.

SIMILAR TO *Raspailia hispida* has a similar branching pattern, but a hispid surface.

Adreus fascicularis. Stoke Point, Devon.

Adreus fascicularis. Lyme Bay, Devon/Dorset.

Raspailia hispida (Montagu, 1814)

Raspailia hispida with a layer of silt. Kimmeridge, Dorset.

A tall (up to around 30cm) mustard yellow, branching sponge with thin (4–6mm) branches which are roughly circular in cross section. The branches tend to taper to points. The branching pattern is variable: some specimens may have many branches immediately out of the basal stalk, but more typically 1–3 branches arise from the base and these may be sparsely branched themselves. The surface of the sponge is hispid (from projecting spicules) and may trap a layer of silt so the sponge can be quite dirty looking. The oscules form evenly spaced rows along branches. This species does not produce slime when taken from the water.

Found on horizontal and vertical bedrock, and on boulders. Usually at sites with some current or wave exposure.

Common on western coasts of Britain, and western and northern Ireland.

KEY FEATURES Tall mustard yellow branching sponge.

SIMILAR TO Can be confused with *Stelligera stuposa*, but is typically taller and less branched. Microscopic examination may be needed to distinguish small specimens of *R. hispida* from large *S. stuposa*.

Raspailia hispida. Rathlin Island, Co. Antrim.

Stelligera stuposa (Ellis & Solander, 1786)

Stelligera stuposa. Rathlin Island, Co. Antrim.

A short mustard yellow branching sponge (normally up to around 10cm tall but may be more). Typically several stubby, slightly flattened in cross section, branches arise immediately from the basal stalk. These may be branched themselves, usually just once, but in taller specimens several levels of branching may occur, typically in all one plane. The surface of the sponge is slimy and hispid (from projecting spicules) and often traps a lot of silt. Small oscules are in groups near the branch tips. The sponge exudes a lot of slime if removed from the water.

On bedrock and boulders, particularly in the circalittoral.

Common on western and channel coasts of Britain and northern and western Ireland.

KEY FEATURES Mustard yellow sponge with short stubby branches.

SIMILAR TO *Raspailia hispida* can look similar, but is typically taller and more branched. Microscopic examination may be needed to distinguish small specimens of *R. hispida* from large *S. stuposa*.

Stelligera stuposa.

Homaxinella subdola (Bowerbank, 1866)

Homaxinella subdola showing untidy appearance from secondary branching. Lundy, Devon.

The clean velvety surface of *Homaxinella subdola*. Isles of Scilly, Cornwall.

A golden yellow, occasionally pale yellow or orange, branched sponge, usually between 4 and 15cm in height. Branches arise irregularly from the main stem and may be twisted and secondarily branched (often at right-angles), giving the sponge an untidy appearance. The sponge has a thin, wiry stem. The branches usually have pointed tips and, unlike many other branched species, a clean velvety surface.

Found on horizontal bedrock in sheltered and slightly exposed conditions.

Only found on south and west coasts of Britain and Ireland – recent records are from the Isles of Scilly, south-west Wales, Cornwall and Devon.

KEY FEATURES Yellow, untidily branched, sponge.

SIMILAR TO *Adreus fascicularis* is typically less branched, may have brown patches on its branches and has a striated appearance.

Axinella dissimilis has a similar colour and surface texture, but has fewer, thicker branches and no secondary branching.

Stelligera montagui

(Montagu, 1814)

The spicule projections that give *Stelligera montagui* a spiky appearance are clearly visible. Rathlin Island, Co. Antrim.

A mustard to pale orange, short (up to 5cm high) branching sponge. The branches are in several planes, very short, and webbed together along their length. Sometimes they are completely fused, so that the sponge can look like a lobed lump, rather than distinctly branched. The spicule projections are quite long, giving the sponge a very spiky appearance – like a bright yellow cactus. Silt is often trapped on the sponge surface on the spicules and in crevices between lobes/branches. This species produces some slime when removed from water.

Found on bedrock and boulders. Usually at sheltered locations with some current.

Common on western and Channel coasts of Britain and around northern and western Ireland.

KEY FEATURES Mustard yellow small sponge with webbed branches.

SIMILAR TO *Axinella damicornis* is similar in form to lobed specimens, but is bright sulphur yellow rather than orangey and much less spiky. Small *S. stuposa* also look similar, but typically have longer branches and are less spiky.

Stelligera montagui specimen with fused branches. Strangford Lough, Co. Down.

Raspailia ramosa Chocolate Finger Sponge (Montagu, 1818)

Raspailia ramosa with obvious oscules. Sunderland, Tyne and Wear.

The very stubby brain-like version of *Raspailia ramosa* common on the east coast. Norfolk.

A chocolate to dark brown branching sponge with many short, thick (up to 1cm diameter), branches arising from a short basal stalk. Some of the branches may be secondarily branched. Branches are roughly circular in cross section with rounded tips. The sponge is hispid and often densely covered in silt. Typically small oscules are visible as clear dark circles in the silt, evenly spread down the branches.

Common on sublittoral rock from exposed to sheltered sites – the only *Raspailia* species known from harbours.

More common on western coasts of Britain and Ireland but there are some recent records from the North Sea.

KEY FEATURES Chocolate brown to dark brown branching sponge.

SIMILAR TO Distinguished from other branching sponges by its dark brown colour. However, there are other rare *Raspailia* species for which the appearance is not known.

Raspailia ramosa. Lyme Bay, Devon/Dorset.

Axinella damicornis Crumpled Duster Sponge (Esper, 1794)

Axinella damicornis growing in association with the anemone *Parazoanthus axinellae*. Prawle Point, Devon.

CW

BP

Axinella damicornis. Rathlin Island, Co. Antrim.

A bright yellow sponge with a distinctive mealy surface. It has many short branches, at all angles, webbed together. Often this gives the overall appearance of a small ball with a folded surface – like a crumpled duster. However, less branched specimens can be fan-like in appearance. Oscules are present on the tips of the branches, and stand out from the sponge surface like short tassels.

Found on bedrock and boulders in both sheltered and exposed locations. Can tolerate some silt.

A southern species at the northern extent of its distribution in Britain and Ireland. Found on southern and western coasts with records from south-west England, Wales, western Scotland and northern and western Ireland.

KEY FEATURES Bright yellow, mealy surfaced sponge with short, fused, branches.

SIMILAR TO *Stelligera montagui* may have a similar form, but is a more muted colour and does not have such obvious oscules or a mealy surface.

Molecular work has recently shown that this species probably belongs to a different genus, *Hymerhabdia*. However, the classification is still being formalised.

Endectyon delaubenfelsi

A darker-coloured specimen of *Endectyon delaubenfelsi* showing flattened branches and the basal stalk. Isles of Scilly, Cornwall.

Yellow ochre or golden, small (to about 6.5cm), branched sponge, rather tree-like in appearance with a thin basal stalk. The flattened branches are usually in one plane and fused together to form fan-like blades. The sponge surface is bumpy and shaggy in appearance.

This is a rare species found on deeper circalittoral bedrock from about 25m depth.

This species was originally described from Plymouth and has recently been recorded from Devon, Lundy and the Scilly Isles. It is also abundant at some sites in the Channel Islands. Further Seasearch records (preferably with photos) would be very useful.

KEY FEATURES Yellow ochre, small, fan-like sponge.

SIMILAR TO *Stelligera montagui* and *Axinella dissimilis* are slightly similar, but the former is more bush-like, with branching in several planes, and the latter is much larger and has a smooth velvety surface and thicker branches.

A small specimen of *Endectyon delaubenfelsi*. Sark, Channel Islands.

Cup / vase / fan

Axinella infundibuliformis Prawn Cracker Sponge (Linnaeus, 1759)

A lobed specimen of *Axinella infundibuliformis*. Firth of Lorn, Argyll and Bute.

Axinella infundibuliformis. Rathlin Island, Co. Antrim.

Typically this sponge is a funnel shape, attached at the base. However, it can grow out from the attachment point in a 90° fan, in the form of a spiral or a cup, or sometimes has lobes. It is normally buff coloured, but can sometimes be a paler whitish-yellow. The edge of the sponge is thick and rounded. Small pores are visible on its surface and sometimes silt and other detritus may adhere to it. The size is very variable, but large specimens may reach about 20cm maximum diameter.

Normally found on bedrock or boulders in the circalittoral.

Widespread on western coasts of Britain and Ireland. Can be very common in some areas. There is a validated record from Northumberland.

Its scientific name comes from the Latin 'infundibuliformis' meaning funnel-formed.

KEY FEATURES Buff funnel or fan-shaped sponge with a rounded edge.

SIMILAR TO *Phakellia ventilabrum* can have a similar form but has a sharp edge and is typically paler in colour.

Phakellia ventilabrum

(Linnaeus, 1767)

A cup-shaped specimen of *Phakellia ventilabrum*. Gigha, Argyll and Bute.

A cup- or fan-shaped sponge attached by a narrow base. The colour is pale grey to cream, and the edge of the sponge is sharp not rounded.

A deeper water species found down to 200m – normally found by divers in slightly sheltered conditions close to deep water.

Most recent records are from western Scotland, particularly sea lochs, others from northern and western Ireland.

KEY FEATURES Pale grey to cream fan or cup-shaped sponge with a sharp edge.

SIMILAR TO *Axinella infundibuliformis* can have a similar form, but has a rounded edge and is normally a more yellow colour.

A fan-shaped specimen of *Phakellia ventilabrum*. Gigha, Argyll and Bute.

Clathria barleei (Bowerbank, 1866)

Fan-shaped specimens of *Clathria barleei*.
Above: The Maidens, Co. Antrim.
Left: Gigha, Argyll and Bute.

The typical form is a cream to pale yellow irregular blade or fan, joined by a wide base to bedrock from which it sticks out at an angle. However, it can also have flattened branches. The surface of the sponge has an irregular pattern of pores and veins. The edge of the fan is translucent with sparse oscules spread along it. This sponge also has an encrusting form which cannot be readily identified without microscopic examination.

This is a rare, northern species usually recorded in water greater than 40m in depth.

There are recent records from the west coast of Scotland and western and northern Ireland.

KEY FEATURES Cream or pale yellow fan-shaped sponge. Typically >40m depth.

SIMILAR TO *Phakellia ventilabrum* and *Axinella infundibuliformis* may form similar fan structures, but do not have veins and pores on their surface or a translucent edge.

A large specimen of *Clathria barleei*. Loch Maddy, Sutherland.

Axinella flustra

The surface oscules are particularly clear on this specimen of *Axinella flustra*. Sark, Channel Islands.

A branched specimen of *Axinella flustra*. Isles of Scilly, Cornwall.

This sponge is beige to yellow in colour, and takes the form of a small blade or fan-shape attached by a stalk to the substrate. Its surface is mealy in texture and has small oscules with channels surrounding them.

Found on exposed coasts on circalittoral bedrock.

Only known from a few sites on western and southern coasts of Britain and Ireland (Aran Islands, Kerry Head Shoals, Scilly Isles, Channel Isles). Further records would be very welcome.

KEY FEATURES Small, fan-shaped, sponge with a mealy surface texture.

SIMILAR TO Unlikely to be confused with other species in Britain and Ireland. *Endectyon teissieri* (not described here) has a similar appearance but is currently known only from French coasts.

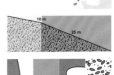

A fan-shaped specimen of *Axinella flustra*. Isles of Scilly, Cornwall.

Spongionella pulchella (Sowerby, 1804)

Spongionella pulchella. The Maidens, Co. Antrim.

A pale green, yellow, grey or buff sponge, sometimes branched but usually in the form of a thick plate with a small stalked base. Also found as small cushions. The sponge surface bears regular conules, and oscules 0.5–1.5mm in diameter are set in depressions over the surface. In fan formed specimens, there is a series of regularly spaced oscules along the top edge. The sponge does not have spicules and has an elastic texture.

This is a scarce species usually found on rock in deeper water (down to 200m) and in moderate or strong tidal streams.

It is widespread in Britain and Ireland with recent records from Shetland, south Wales and the English Channel. The majority of records are from Northern Ireland's east coast (this possibly reflects increased survey effort).

The scientifc name comes from the Latin 'pulchella' meaning pretty.

KEY FEATURES Pale yellow, green or buff sponge usually in the form of a stalked plate with oscules along one edge.

SIMILAR TO *Dysidea fragilis* also has a conulose surface but with more pronounced conules, and normally grows as a thick cushion.

Haliclona urceolus (Rathke & Vahl, 1806)

A single tube specimen of *Halilcona urceolus*. Loch Fyne, Highland.

This sponge is in the form of one or more cylinders, each normally bearing a terminal oscule (some blind tubes do occur), attached to the substrate by a thin stalk. Frequently the sponge consists of only one cylinder, but in some specimens several may be joined onto one stalk and these can be branched. The colour is pale yellow to light brown. Specimens can be up to 15cm in height but are frequently smaller.

Found from the infralittoral to 1,000m on stone and bedrock in both sheltered and exposed habitats.

All coasts of Britain and Ireland, but most frequent in north-west Scotland and north-east Ireland.

KEY FEATURES Stalked pale yellow to brown cylindrical sponge with terminal oscule.

SIMILAR TO The top cylinder can look similar to other *Haliclona* species, but these lack the thin stalk.

Three specimens of *Haliclona urceolus*, two single tubes (left) and one branched. Loch Long, Argyll and Bute.

Tubular

Sycon ciliatum Purse Sponge
(Fabricius, 1780)

The hairy surface and fringe of spines around the terminal oscule are clearly visible in both images. Left: Sark, Channel Islands. Right: Poole Bay, Dorset.

A small pale brown, greyish or cream, cylindrical, calcareous sponge usually between 1 and 3cm in length but can be up to 9cm. The cylinder is attached by one end and open at the other with a terminal oscule with a fringe of spines. The whole surface of the sponge is covered in spines giving it a hairy and often, as they collect silt, a rather dirty appearance. Specimens can vary quite considerably in appearance and it is probable this is a species complex. Often solitary, but sometimes individuals occur in clusters.

Found most often on the shore and in the shallow sublittoral, often attached to seaweed. Also sublittorally in a variety of habitats.

Found on all coasts of Britain and Ireland.

KEY FEATURES Cream to grey tubular sponge with a hairy surface and a fringe of spines around the open end.

SIMILAR TO *Grantia compressa* is similar in appearance but flattened, and has a smooth rather than hairy surface.

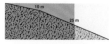

Leucosolenia spp. Spiky Lace Sponge

The overall spiky appearance of a *Leucosolenia* sp. colony. Swanage Bay, Dorset.

Leucosolenia sp. clearly showing the oscules at the ends of the tubes, and a single specimen of *Sycon ciliatum* at the bottom of the colony. Loch Hourn, Highland.

A white or grey sponge composed of many thin tubes. The basal tubes cling onto the substrate and from these, numerous short, sometimes branched, tubes arise. Each of the tubes bears a terminal oscule.

Found from the shore, where it may be common under overhangs, into deeper water on shells, sea squirts, seaweed and bedrock.

Found on all coasts of Britain and Ireland.

KEY FEATURES Spiky white to grey sponge with many short projecting tubes.

SIMILAR TO The protruding tubes give this genus a spiky appearance which is distinctive from other local *Calcarea* species.

Considerable taxonomic confusion in the genus *Leucosolenia* means that spicule form and external appearance are not well known for local species (including *Leucosolenia botryoides* (Ellis & Solander, 1786), *L. variabilis* Haeckel, 1870 and *L. complicata* (Montagu, 1818)). Defining field and laboratory characteristics for identification will require much taxonomic revision so, until this work is done it is safest to record as *Leucosolenia* sp.

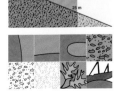

Grantia compressa Compressed Purse Sponge (Fabricius, 1780)

Many specimens of *Grantia compressa* growing on the hydroid *Sertularia argentea*. Menai Strait, Anglesey.

A cream or greyish calcareous sponge with a smooth, clean surface. The form of the body is, as the English name suggests, like a small oval purse with an oscule opening at the top end. Frequently several sponges occur together in a small cluster.

Found from the shore, under overhangs and boulders, into the shallow sublittoral where it is often attached to algae.

Common on all British and Irish coasts.

KEY FEATURES Cream or grey, smooth, flattened purse-shaped sponge.

SIMILAR TO *Sycon ciliatum* is a similar size but not flattened, tends to be darker grey-brown in colour with a bristly surface and its terminal oscule is fringed by a ring of spicules.

Grantia compressa.
Swanage, Dorset.

Clathrina coriacea White Lace Sponge (Montagu, 1814)

Clathrina coriacea is often found in association with the sea squirt *Dendrodoa grossularia*. Isle of Man.

Clathrina coriacea. Loch Hourn, Highland.

A delicate, normally white (but can be grey, pale rose, pale yellow, orange, or lemon yellow) calcareous encrusting sponge found attached onto bedrock in thin patches. The patches are very variable in size from 1–2 cm to around 30cm. The sponge is formed of a mesh of thin tubes (~1mm in diameter) which often form small mounds each topped with an oscule. This can give the whole sponge an overall spiky appearance.

Often found in association with the sea squirt *Dendrodoa grossularia* in tide swept areas or surge gullies, but also occurs in sheltered habitats such as caves and overhangs.

Found from the lower shore, where it is often hidden under boulders, into the circalittoral, although most common in shallow waters.

Widespread and common in Britain and Ireland

KEY FEATURES White, delicate, spiky-looking, encrusting sponge composed of intertwined thin tubes.

SIMILAR TO The sponges *Clathrina lacunosa* and *Leucosolenia* spp. are also formed of thin tubes. *Clathrina lacunosa* can be easily distinguished as it is stalked. Local *Leucosolenia* species tend to form oval balls rather than crusts and are rather bushy in appearance with many protruding tubes. Some bryozoans are similar in appearance but are hard. There are several other *Clathrina* species which are similar in appearance but at present most of these are not thought to occur in Britain and Ireland. However, further study is likely to show that what we currently call different forms of *Clathrina coriacea* are actually several distinct species.

Globular

Clathrina lacunosa (Johnston, 1842)

Three specimens of *Clathrina lacunosa*. Rathlin Island, Co. Antrim.

Clathrina lacunosa. Pembrokeshire.

Small, white, ball-shaped, calcareous sponge with a thin stalk. The whole sponge is usually under 3cm in height with the ball under 1cm in diameter. The ball is composed of tightly intertwined tubes but the stalk is solid.

Grows on bedrock and, particularly in sheltered sealochs. May grow on empty shells, hydroids or bryozoans.

Recorded from the shore to depths of over 600m. Fairly common but often overlooked because of its small size so there are comparatively few records.

Widely reported from western coasts of Britain and Ireland. Less common from the east coast but has been found recently in Essex and County Durham.

Previously known as *Guancha lacunosa*.

KEY FEATURES Very small stalked ball composed of intertwined tubes.

SIMILAR TO Can be distinguished from most other calcareous sponges by its thin stalk. *Clathrina blanca* (Miklucho-Maclay, 1868) (not described here) is reported from the Arctic and Norway to the Azores and Mediterranean, including Britain and Ireland, and can only be distinguished by examining its spicules – external characteristics for this species are not well known. The sea squirt *Bolteniopsis prenanti* may appear superficially similar but does not have the textured surface of *C. lacunosa*.

Tethya citrina Golf Ball Sponge Sarà & Melone, 1965

This specimen of *Tethya citrina* is producing reproductive buds that will eventually break off and become new specimens. Llŷn Peninsula, Gwynedd.

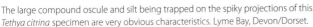

The large compound oscule and silt being trapped on the spiky projections of this *Tethya citrina* specimen are very obvious characteristics. Lyme Bay, Devon/Dorset.

A ball shaped yellow or orange sponge covered in spiky projections. The spikes often have small buds on their ends. These projections trap silt, with some specimens almost entirely covered. A large compound oscule is usually present near the top of the sponge.

Found on horizontal or sloping rock surfaces from the intertidal down to 930m.

Common on western and southern coasts of Britain and Ireland but absent from the North Sea. Britain and Ireland are at the northern end of its distribution.

Specimens from Britain and Ireland were formerly known as *Tethya aurantium* (Pallas, 1766), but studies have shown that this species is probably restricted to the Mediterranean.

KEY FEATURES Ball-shaped yellow sponge with spiky projections covering its surface.

SIMILAR TO Small specimens could be confused with the sponges *Tethya hibernica* Heim, Nickel, Picton & Brümmer, 2007 or *Tethya norvegica* Bowerbank, 1872 (none of which are described here). It would require examination of spicules to confirm identification. Large specimens may be initially mistaken for *Suberites carnosus* but that species has a smooth surface.

Suberites carnosus (Johnston, 1842)

Three specimens of *Suberites carnosus*. These individuals have a varying number of oscules. Mullaghmore, Co. Sligo.

Suberites carnosus, note the large single oscule. Strangford Lough, Co. Down.

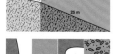

A ball-shaped buff, or pale orange, yellow or brown coloured sponge, often with a large compound oscule at its top. Attached onto bedrock by a short stalk.

Found on horizontal bedrock or attached to stones or shells in muddy areas. Tolerant of silt.

Common around Ireland and on western coasts of Britain, occasional records from the North Sea.

The scientific name 'carnosus' comes from the Latin meaning fleshy, which could describe its texture or colour.

KEY FEATURES Spherical sponge with a smooth surface and often one large oscule on top.

SIMILAR TO *Tethya citrina* has a spiky or knobbly surface and is usually much brighter in colour. *Suberites ficus* looks similar, but is usually composed of several lobes and is a much brighter orange in colour.

Quasillina brevis (Bowerbank, 1861)

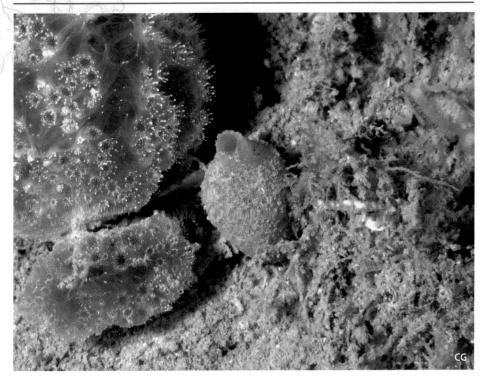

Small specimen of *Quasillina brevis* next to the sea squirt *Sidynum elegans*. Isles of Scilly, Cornwall.

Small stalked pale orange sponge with an oval bladder-like body up to 5.5cm high and 2.5cm wide. There is a single oscule on the top of the sponge, slightly elevated as a more transparent structure.

Found on bedrock from 15–700m in depth.

Rarely reported from shallow water in Britain and Ireland. Recent records are from south-west Ireland and the Isles of Scilly; additional records would be very welcome.

The scientific name 'brevis' comes from the Latin for short, and refers to the short length of its stalk which almost completely merges into the main sponge body.

KEY FEATURES Small stalked sponge with oval body and single terminal oscule.

SIMILAR TO Unlikely to be confused with any other species.

Thinly encrusting

Terpios gelatinosus (Bowerbank, 1866)

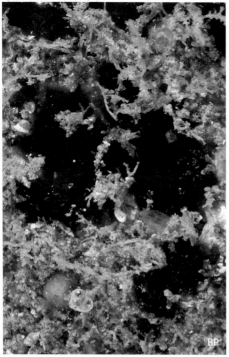

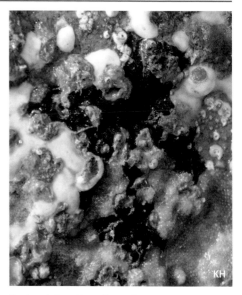

Terpios gelatinosa. Looe, Cornwall.

Terpios gelatinosa. Red Flag Island, Kilkieran Bay, Co. Galway.

Very thinly encrusting dark or royal blue sponge. This sponge is actually yellow or orange, but the colour is transformed by symbiotic algae in its tissues.

Found under boulders on the shore and in the shallow sublittoral in areas of strong water movement. Also in caves.

Common on the south coast of England and in Wales. Found as far north as Scotland all around Britain and Ireland.

In much older literature it is listed as *Terpios fugax* Duchassaing & Michelotti, 1864, but this Caribbean species, although very similar in appearance, is not likely to occur in Europe.

KEY FEATURES Very thin dark blue encrusting sponge.

SIMILAR TO The only other blue sponge likely to be seen by divers is *Hymedesmia paupertas* – this is typically a paler blue or blue-green and has prominent pore sieves on its surface. Some specimens of *T. gelatinosa* may be yellow or green rather than the typical blue. These are impossible to distinguish from other encrusting species without examining their spicules.

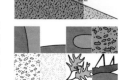

Halisarca dujardinii

Halisarca dujardinii on the underside of an intertidal boulder. Penzance, Cornwall.

Slimy greyish-yellow sponge which forms small patches up to around 5cm in diameter, either as thin sheets or low cushions.

A common shore species which is found under boulders mid-shore, and under overhangs and on seaweed and kelp holdfasts on the lower shore. Also found in the subtidal down to at least 50m.

Found on all coasts of Britain and Ireland.

KEY FEATURES Encrusting grey-yellow sponge typically found under boulders on the shore.

SIMILAR TO Can be confused with other yellow encrusting sponges – most likely *Hymedesmia brondstedi* (not described here) which can also be common on the shore. *H. brondstedi* typically has channels on its surface. If in doubt microscopic examination may be required – *H. dujardinii* has no spicules.

Oscarella sp. occurs in similar habitats but has small lobes on its surface.

Some encrusting colonial sea squirts may be superficially similar.

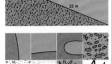

Oscarella sp.

Oscarella sp., Jersey, Channel Islands.

A pale yellow specimen of *Oscarella* sp. Kimmeridge, Dorset.

Thinly encrusting pale yellow to red sponge. The surface is distinctively thrown up into a series of bubbles or drip like projections, each up to 1cm in diameter. Sometimes the sponge incorporates algae into its tissue and then may have patches of pink to dark red. Individuals can form very large sheets.

Found from the shore, under boulders, to depths of 300m, encrusting on bedrock or boulders.

Common in Britain and Ireland.

KEY FEATURES Pale yellow to red encrusting sponge with distinctive bubble-like projections on its surface.

SIMILAR TO Local specimens of *Oscarella* have recently been split from Mediterranean species including *Oscarella lobularis* using molecular techniques and advanced microscopy – these species are currently impossible to separate using external morphology alone and therefore we recommend recording as *Oscarella* sp. Can be confused with *Halisarca dujardinii* when out of water as the bubbles collapse and the two species are similar in colour.

Oscarella sp. under an intertidal boulder. Strangford Lough, Co. Down.

Ophlitaspongia papilla

Ophlitaspongia papilla on the underside of an intertidal boulder. Strangford Lough, Co. Down.

Dark orange-red encrusting sponge with large regular round oscules fairly evenly spaced, 5–10mm apart, over its surface. Normally a thin 2–3mm deep crust but sometimes forms cushions up to 10mm thick.

Present on the lower shore and down to around 5m sublittorally in areas of strong wave or tidal water movement. Under boulders on the shore and growing on rock or seaweed in the sublittoral.

Found on all British and Irish coasts.

KEY FEATURES Red-orange encrusting species with large, evenly spaced, round oscules. Found on the lower shore and in very shallow water.

SIMILAR TO Not many other red-orange encrusting species are found in a similar habitat. *Clathria (Microciona) atrasanguinea* (Bowerbank, 1862) (not described here) is another orange encrusting species, but crumbles and tears when removed from the rock whereas *O. papilla* usually comes off in sheets. *Amphilectus fucorum* can be distinguished by its distinctive smell when fresh and orange rather than red-orange colour. Both of the above species lack the characteristic round, evenly spaced, oscules.

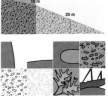

Dercitus bucklandi Black Tar Sponge (Bowerbank, 1858)

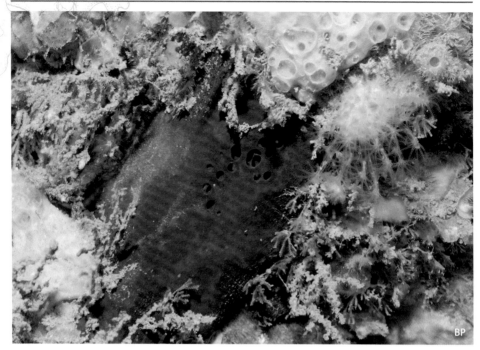

Dercitus bucklandi. Rathlin Island, Co. Antrim.

A very distinctive black encrusting sponge with the appearance of stretched, slightly folded rubber. The dull surface has patches of large oscules on it, normally towards the centre of the sponge.

Found stretched across crevices on vertical and overhanging bedrock.

South-western distribution in Britain and Ireland.

KEY FEATURES Black encrusting sponge with appearance like stretched rubber.

SIMILAR TO Could possibly be confused with a very dark specimen of *Pachymatisma johnstonia*. There are no other black sponges found in Britain and Ireland.

Dercitus bucklandi. Rathlin Island, Co. Antrim.

Leuconia nivea showing oscules at the top of the surface ridges. Swanage, Dorset.

Leuconia nivea. Pembrokeshire.

White to pale grey, encrusting, hard, calcareous sponge. It forms a thin sheet or low cushion with the smooth, clean, surface thrown up into low ridges and mounds. Oscules sparsely scattered on top of ridges.

Very common on the lower shore and shallow subtidal (but also reported to 128m), especially in areas of strong tidal movement.

Present on all British and Irish coasts.

Its name comes from the Latin 'niveus', meaning snow.

KEY FEATURES Hard, white sponge with folded surface.

SIMILAR TO Can be confused with *Leuconia johnstoni* Carter, 1871 (not described here). However *L. johnstoni* has a dirty appearance as it traps silt, and is shaped like a cluster of *Sycon ciliatum*.

Encrusting – spiky

Tethyspira spinosa (Bowerbank, 1874)

Salmon pink massive specimen of *Tethyspira spinosa*. Pembrokeshire.

An encrusting sponge varying from cream, pale-pink to peachy-orange in colour. Form can be thickly encrusting but often the sponge is in a low mound. The surface texture is very distinctive with projecting columns of spicules raising it into conules and projecting to form bristles. Often these bristles are covered in silt so the sponge can appear rather dirty. Some specimens also have large transparent oscules.

On wave exposed bedrock from the shallow subtidal down to at least 60m.

This species has a predominantly south-western distribution in Britain and Ireland, with recent records from western Scotland, Rathlin Island, Wales, Lundy, Devon, and Cornwall and the Isles of Scilly.

KEY FEATURES Cream, pink or orange thickly encrusting sponge with distinctive conulose surface.

SIMILAR TO *Dysidea fragilis* may look similar to white specimens but lacks the bristle-like projections of *T. spinosa*.

Cream encrusting, specimen of *Tethyspira spinosa*. Sanda Sound, Argyll and Bute.

Dysidea fragilis Goosebump Sponge (Montagu, 1818)

Dysidea fragilis showing the conulose surface and white coloration. Selsey, Sussex.

A grey-white specimen of *Dysidea fragilis*. Swanage Pier, Dorset.

A white to grey sponge with a strongly conulose surface, resembling goose bumps. Forms cushions, or sometimes thick crusts, which may have lobe or finger projections. Scattered oscules which are variable in size. Cushions usually less than 15cm in diameter.

On bedrock and boulders from the intertidal down to the circalittoral. Tolerates some silt.

Common on all coasts of Britain and Ireland.

KEY FEATURES White or grey encrusting sponge with strongly conulose surface.

SIMILAR TO *Dysidea pallescens* (Schmidt, 1862) (not described here) has also been recorded from several locations around Britain and Ireland. This has a similar surface appearance to *D. fragilis*, but is pink-purple in colour and tends to have large oscules. *Ulosa digitata* can sometimes resemble *D. fragilis*, although is usually a reddish colour rather than white. Examination of the skeleton under a microscope may be needed to distinguish any specimens which have an unusual appearance.

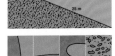

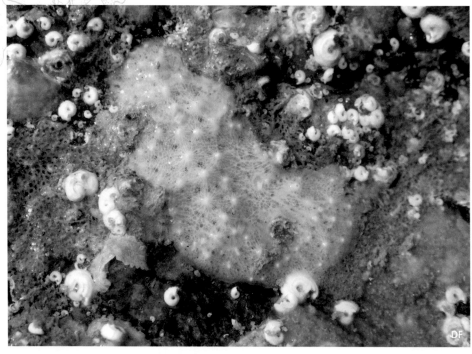

Aplysilla sulfurea under an intertidal boulder. Marazion, Cornwall.

Aplysilla sulfurea and *A. rosea* (opposite) form crusts with their surface bearing distinctive short spiky projections. These conules are typically around 0.5mm high and spaced 0.8–1.6mm apart. Patches are typically relatively small – up to 40mm in extent and 5mm in thickness. They may bear oscules raised up on chimneys and ostia are sometimes visible as small dots in between the conules. *A. sulfurea* is a bright sulphur yellow.

Schulze when describing *A. sulfurea* and *A. rosea* could not decide if they were distinct species or colour morphs of the same species as structurally they are very similar (as this species lacks spicules there is not much to go on!).

Typically found out of bright light – under boulders on the shore and in caves and under overhangs sublittorally down to 320m (*A. sulfurea*).

A. sulfurea has a similar distribution to *A. rosea*, but is more frequently recorded and there are a couple of records from the east coast of Britain. Both species are likely to be under-recorded due to the small patch sizes and cryptic habitat.

KEY FEATURES Encrusting yellow sponge with strongly conulose surface.

SIMILAR TO The combination of the bright yellow colour and the spiky surface appearance is unlikely to be confused with any other British or Irish sponges.

Aplysilla rosea (Barrois, 1876)

Aplysilla rosea. Kimmeridge, Dorset.

Aplysilla rosea is visually very similar to *A. sulfurea* (opposite) except in colour, being a deep rose pink. It is found in identical habitats to *A. sulfurea* but occurs at greater depths sublittorally (640m). *A. rosea* has been recorded from southern and western coasts of Britain and Ireland.

KEY FEATURES Encrusting pink sponge with strongly conulose surface.

SIMILAR TO The combination of the pink colour and the spiky surface appearance is unlikely to be confused with any other British or Irish sponges. *Chelonaplysilla noevus* (Carter, 1876) (not described here) also has conules but is a darker purple colour and has a reticulation of sand grains visible on its surface.

A maroon specimen of *Aplysilla rosea*. The Maidens, Co. Antrim.

Massive / thickly encrusting

Haliclona viscosa Volcano Sponge (Topsent, 1888)

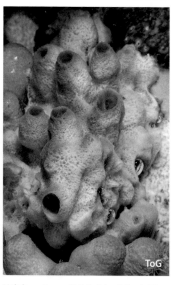

Haliclona viscosa with prominent volcano-like mounds bearing terminal oscules. Isles of Scilly, Cornwall.

Haliclona viscosa. Rathlin Island, Co. Antrim.

A thickly encrusting to massive sponge with surface bearing mounds, each with a terminal oscule. In encrusting specimens the mounds may be low and rounded, but in larger specimens the long projections with a bumpy surface do resemble volcanic craters. There are beige and purple colour forms. Specimens may reach over 40cm in diameter. Produces a lot of slime when broken and may feel slimy if touched.

Found from the infralittoral to 50m on rock in areas with current and low turbidity.

Present on all coasts of Britain and Ireland but more common on western coasts.

KEY FEATURES Massive beige or purple sponge with volcano-like mounds bearing terminal oscules.

SIMILAR TO *Haliclona cinerea* also can be purple with mounds. However, a network of fibres is usually visible on its surface and the lobes tend to be smaller and more even.

A beige specimen of *Haliclona viscosa*. Firth of Lorn, Argyll and Bute.

Haliclona cinerea (Grant, 1826)

Haliclona cinerea. Strangford Lough, Co. Down.

Haliclona cinerea, close-up showing the surface mesh of spongin fibres. Strangford Lough, Co. Down.

Massively encrusting sponge usually with several mounds on its surface, each topped with a large oscule. The surface appearance is very distinctive as a disordered network of criss-crossed spongin fibres is clearly visible through the outer surface. There are two colour forms: beige to pale peach or yellow, and pale to dark purple. Sometimes the sponge forms branches. Under boulders on the lower shore, the sponge is usually thinly encrusting, although the fibre network is still visible. The sponge forms slime strands if torn.

In the shallow sublittoral, particularly areas with currents. May also be found under boulders on the lower shore.

All coasts of Britain and Ireland from Shetland to the Isles of Scilly.

KEY FEATURES Beige or pink-purple encrusting sponge with oscules raised on chimneys and spongin fibre network visible through sponge surface.

SIMILAR TO The subtidal mounded form is unlikely to be confused with anything else. Intertidal specimens may be confused with *Haliclona rosea* (Bowerbank, 1866) (not described here) or, if purple, *Haliclona viscosa*. Those two species can normally be distinguished as they lack visible fibres. However, microscopic examination of the skeleton may be required for definitive identification.

Suberites ficus Sea Orange (Johnston, 1842)

Suberites ficus, large many-lobed specimen. The orange is the usual colour and the green patches are due to symbiotic algae in the tissues. Far Mulberry, Selsey, Sussex.

A large, smooth sponge composed of several lobes. Often with several large oscules irregularly dispersed but usually near the top of the lobes. Can occur growing on scallops and shells. However, these specimens are not identifiable without examining their spicules as they could be confused with other orange encrusting species.

Found in sheltered waters, particularly those with tidal currents on rock, wreckage or attached to shells or pebbles in silty areas. Can also be found loose lying amongst algae in sheltered sites.

All coasts of Britain and Ireland.

KEY FEATURES Large orange sponge with a velvety surface and large, irregularly distributed, oscules.

SIMILAR TO Small specimens composed of one or two lobes may be confused with *Suberites carnosus*, but this species is typically a much paler buff or yellow colour.

This sponge growing on the shell of a scallop required microscopic examination to confirm the species as *S. ficus*. Loch Melfort, Firth of Lorn, Argyll and Bute.

Suberites massa

Suberites massa Nardo, 1847

MM

A large multi-lobed specimen (above) and a smaller version (left) of *Suberites massa*. Both images Poole Harbour, Dorset.

LB

Yellow-orange sponge with many small lobes. Often covered in silt so only the tips of the lobes are exposed. Up to 30cm diameter and 10cm thick, but smaller fist sized specimens are more typical. Larger specimens are similar in appearance to a human brain.

Found on shells, boulders and sea walls in silty, brackish, waters of harbour, estuaries and lagoons where there are moderate tidal currents.

In Britain was previously only known along the channel coast in the Fleet and Poole Harbour (Dorset), Southampton Water (Hampshire) and Plymouth Sound (Devon). However, there are recent Seasearch records from Essex and Kent. Apparently absent from Ireland. A southern species reaching its northern limits in Britain and Ireland.

KEY FEATURES Yellow-orange sponge composed of many small lobes.

SIMILAR TO Not likely to be confused with other sponge species, except possibly a small ragged specimen of *Polymastia boletiformis*. Could possibly be mistaken for a colony of orange sea squirts.

MASSIVE / THICKLY ENCRUSTING 167

Ulosa digitata (Schmidt, 1866)

Ulosa digitata. Mewstone Ledges, Plymouth, Devon.

Ulosa digitata. Plymouth, Devon.

A soft salmon pink crust or thin cushion shaped sponge. The sponge sometimes has digitate projections, and some specimens may even have more pronounced branching. Very conulose surface with quite a hispid appearance.

Found in wave sheltered locations in the infralittoral and sublittoral. Frequently growing on seaweed, but also occurs on rocks. A southern species.

Distribution is not well known and further records are most welcome. Probably restricted to the southern coasts of England in Britain and Ireland.

Previously named *Ulosa stuposa* (Esper, 1794) but the name given by Esper was already in use for a different species and the next available name is *Ulosa digitata*.

KEY FEATURES Pinky-orange or salmon pink crust or cushion with very conulose surface.

SIMILAR TO *Dysidea fragilis* also has a conulose surface, but is white to grey in colour and less ragged looking.

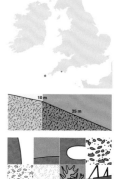

Myxilla incrustans (Johnston, 1842)

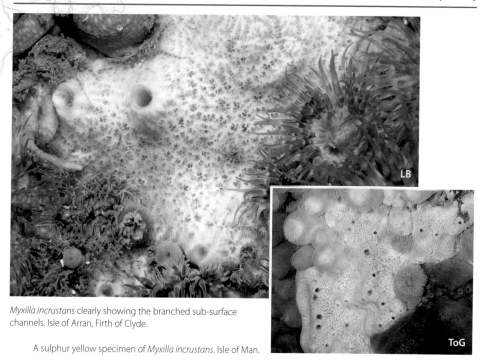

Myxilla incrustans clearly showing the branched sub-surface channels. Isle of Arran, Firth of Clyde.

A sulphur yellow specimen of *Myxilla incrustans*. Isle of Man.

A pale yellow to sulphur yellow thickly encrusting to massive sponge. When massive, it frequently has conical projections or lower mounds topped by large oscules. In encrusting forms, large oscules are spread over its surface. Branched channels visible through the translucent sponge surface produce a distinctive frost or fern-like pattern. The sponge is very slimy if collected.

From the low-water mark into deep water.

All coasts of Britain and Ireland.

KEY FEATURES Yellow massive or thickly encrusting sponge with distinctive pattern of channels on its surface.

SIMILAR TO The massive forms are unlikely to be mistaken for anything else but encrusting forms could be confused with *Myxilla rosacea* or *Myxilla fimbriata* (Bowerbank, 1866) (not described here). However, the latter of those two species is typically orange or peach, and microscopic examination of the spicules would be required to confirm identification.

A large, pale, specimen of *Myxilla incrustans*. Isle of Skye, Highland.

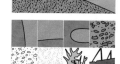

Myxilla rosacea

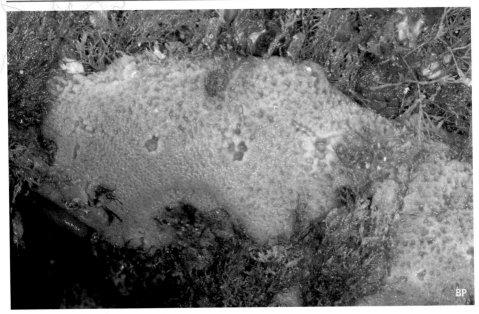

Myxilla rosacea under an intertidal boulder. Strangford Lough, Co. Down.

A cream to pale yellow thickly encrusting sponge. The surface has an irregular pattern of veins and pores and small mounds and projections – giving it an appearance like a scrambled egg.

Found on the shore down to 300m, mainly at exposed sites.

All coasts of Britain and Ireland, more frequent on western coasts but a few records from the North Sea.

KEY FEATURES Cream to pale yellow thickly encrusting sponge with irregular mounds and projections.

SIMILAR TO Could be confused with *Myxilla incrustans*, when thinly encrusting, or *Myxilla fimbriata* (Bowerbank, 1866) (not described here), although the latter species is typically orange or peach. If in doubt, microscopic examination of the spicules would be required to confirm identification.

Myxilla rosacea. Rathlin Island, Co. Antrim.

Pachymatisma johnstonia Elephant Hide Sponge
(Bowerbank in Johnston, 1842)

Typical grey colour form of *Pachymatisma johnstonia*. The purple patches are symbiotic algae growing in the sponge's tissues. Lyme Bay, Devon/Dorset.

A pale grey sponge that forms large, low rounded cushions or lobes on bedrock and stable boulders. Individuals can be very large – some reach over 50cm in diameter. Velvety surface with evenly spaced oscules on top of mounds and ridges.

Found from the intertidal down to 300m.

Common in much of Britain and Ireland. Previously thought to be absent from North Sea coasts, but there are a few recent records from Norfolk, the Farnes, and Aberdeenshire. Specimens previously identified as *P. johnstonia* from Sweden and Norway have been classified as the distinct species *P. normani* so the wider distribution is unclear.

KEY FEATURES Massively encrusting large sponge with a velvety grey surface.

SIMILAR TO Normal grey specimens are unlikely to be mistaken for anything else. However, under overhangs and in caves it can be white, and may then be confused with *Stryphnus ponderosus* (Bowerbank, 1866) or *Stelletta grubii* Schmidt, 1862 (neither species described here).

A pale specimen of *Pachmatisma johnstonia* growing under an overhang. Sanda Sound, Argyll and Bute.

Thymosia guernei Mashed Potato Sponge Topsent, 1895

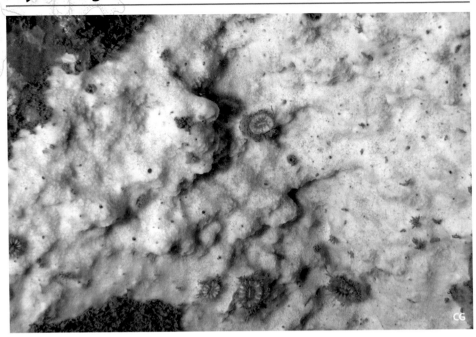

A large patch of *Thymosia guernei* showing the lumpy appearance. Pembrokeshire.

A white to cream sponge with an irregular surface, forming a thick crust or lumpy lobes on rock. Patches up to 60cm in diameter with, as the English name suggests, an overall appearance like cold mashed potato.

Found in crevices and beneath overhangs usually in areas moderately exposed to waves and currents.

A southern species with records in Britain and Ireland from south-west England, the Channel Islands, Lundy, south-west Wales and western and southern coasts of Ireland.

KEY FEATURES Encrusting to massive sponge with the appearance of cold mashed potato.

SIMILAR TO The mashed potato appearance is fairly distinctive – other large, white encrusting sponges usually have a smooth surface.

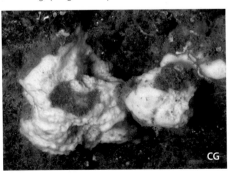

Thymosia guernei.
Plymouth, Devon.

Mycale lingua (Bowerbank, 1866)

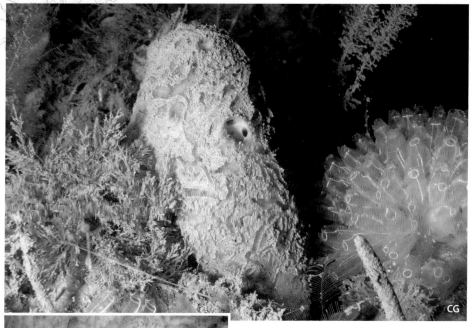

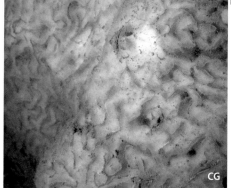

Mycale lingua. Loch Caolisport, Argyll and Bute.

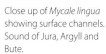

Close up of *Mycale lingua* showing surface channels. Sound of Jura, Argyll and Bute.

Massive cream to pale grey-yellow lump up to 30cm in height. The surface has a distinctive irregular network of angular channels. Large oscules (4–10mm) are scattered irregularly over the sponge. Can be a roundish mound or an erect form with a base narrower than the top. It has been described as resembling the tongue of a sheep: the scientific name comes from the Latin for tongue – 'lingua'.

A deep water species which has only been recorded in the 30–50m range.

Found in a few localities – mainly from western Scotland with additional recent records from Northern Ireland and Bardsey in Wales.

KEY FEATURES Massive cream to pale grey lump with distinctive channels on its surface. Deeper water species (>30m).

SIMILAR TO The channels on the surface are very distinctive, and this species is not likely to be confused with anything else.

Halichondria panicea Breadcrumb Sponge (Pallas, 1766)

A large subtidal specimen of *Halichondria panicea*. Selsey, Sussex.

Very variable in form ranging from thin sheets, to cushions and large branching forms. Cream to yellow in shaded sites, but pale green in well-lit areas owing to the presence of symbiotic algae in its tissues. Oscules can be raised on conules, in regular lines along flat specimens, or on the tips of branches.

One of the most common intertidal and subtidal sponges. Found on all coasts of Britain and Ireland.

The English name comes from the texture of the sponge, like breadcrumbs.

KEY FEATURES Yellow or pale green encrusting sponge with very variable form.

SIMILAR TO Most easily confused with *H. bowerbanki*, and yellow encrusting forms may need microscopic examination to distinguish. However, *H. bowerbanki* is never green in colour and often has tassels.

An intertidal specimen of *Halichondria panicea* showing the prominent regular oscules. Wembury, Devon.

Halichondria bowerbanki

Halichondria bowerbanki growing over the darker orange *Amphilectus fucorum*. Strangford Lough, Co. Down.

This pale yellow or cream sponge varies widely in form. It can be a simple encrusting cushion, but usually specimens have some form of projections; either finger-like with terminal oscules or, more typically, many thin, tassel-like branches. The tassels are often tangled together or around other organisms such as hydroids and bryozoans.

Most abundant in sheltered, silty or estuarine conditions such as harbours. Intertidal or shallow sublittoral.

Common on all coasts of Britain and Ireland.

This sponge was named after the British naturalist and palaeontologist James Scott Bowerbank (1797–1877) who did much of the early work on British and Irish sponges.

KEY FEATURES Cream or yellow sponge, typically with fine tassel-like projections.

SIMILAR TO *H. panicea* is similar, but this species never develops tassel-like branches and is often a greenish-hue in well-lit conditions (*H. bowerbanki* is never green in colour). *H. panicea* does not occur in highly silted conditions.

Tassels are not present all year round in *H. bowerbanki*, and distinction between the two species may require examination of spicules.

Halichondria bowerbanki, in silted conditions. Strangford Lough, Co. Down.

Iophon nigricans   (Bowerbank, 1858)

Iophon nigricans. The Maidens, Co. Antrim.

A thickly encrusting cream to yellow sponge which often bears irregular finger-like projections. The sponge has a fairly soft texture. Oscules can be found along projections or on ridges on mound forms.

The name of this species comes from the fact that when removed from water, after a while, it turns black. This species was formerly known as *lophonopsis nigricans*.

Found on rocks, boulders and shells at sheltered or moderately exposed sites with moderate to strong tidal streams. Normally in the circalittoral (to 108m).

Common in Britain and Ireland.

KEY FEATURES Thickly encrusting cream to yellow sponge, often with irregular finger-like projections.

SIMILAR TO Can be similar in appearance to *lophon hyndmani*. If in doubt microscopic examination will be required to distinguish the two. *Myxilla incrustans* is brighter in colour and has surface channels.

A specimen of *lophon nigricans* with finger-like projections. The Maidens, Co. Antrim.

Iophon hyndmani

(Bowerbank, 1858)

The massive form of *Iophon hyndmani*. The Maidens, Co. Antrim.

The encrusting form of *Iophon hyndmani* with obvious star-shaped vein patterns around the oscules. The Maidens, Co. Antrim.

This pale yellow sponge comes in two growth forms. Often it is thickly encrusting, growing up hydroids and over bryozoans. Typically this gives the overall sponge a bobbly form – rather like popcorn, but it may also have soft, irregular branches. It can also form a thin crust which has distinctive star-shaped vein patterns around its oscules.

Found in both sheltered and exposed waters. Often encrusts shells, hydroids, bryozoans and other sessile organisms but can also be found on bedrock.

Southern and Western coasts of Britain and all coasts of Ireland. No records for east coast of Britain but, particularly the encrusting form, likely to be under-recorded.

KEY FEATURES White to pale yellow sponge which can encrust rock or animals such as hydroids.

SIMILAR TO The erect form can be confused with *I. nigricans* – microscopic examination is required for definitive identification. The encrusting pale yellow form may be very difficult to distinguish from other encrusting species of a similar colour, and will probably require microscopic examination to confirm identification.

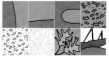

Massive or encrusting – with pore sieves

Hemimycale columella Crater Sponge (Bowerbank, 1874)

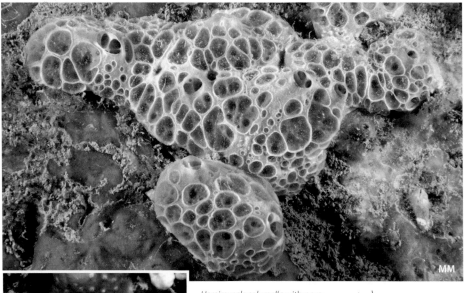

Hemimycale columella with pore sieves expanded. Poole Bay, Dorset.

Hemimycale columella with pore sieves contracted. Rathlin Island, Co. Antrim.

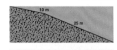

A thickly encrusting peach, salmon pink or pale orange sponge with large oval pore depressions or 'pore sieves' on its surface. The pore sieves are darker than the surface tissue and very closely spaced, almost touching, and this and the fact they often have white rims gives an appearance like honeycomb. Sometimes the pore sieves contract and will then only be visible as slightly paler pimples on the surface.

Found on bedrock and boulders.

Found on all coasts of Britain and Ireland, but rare on North Sea coasts.

KEY FEATURES Peach to pale orange encrusting sponge with large pore sieves that have a dark interior and pale rims.

SIMILAR TO Some species of *Hymedesmia* and *Phorbas* are a similar colour, but their pore sieves are the same colour as the rest of the sponge.

Hymedesmia paupertas (Bowerbank, 1866)

A green-blue specimen of *Hymedesmia paupertas*. Purbeck, Dorset.

Hymedesmia paupertas, green variant. Rathlin Island, Co. Antrim.

A thinly encrusting sponge with raised, circular, pore sieve rims on its surface. Colour can be yellow-green, green, green-blue or bright blue. Patches can be very small (1–2cm diameter) to around 10cm across. Sometimes the pore sieves contract, and then are only visible as small pimples on the sponge surface.

Found on rock down to 400m.

Records from south-west England to the Isle of Wight, Wales, western and northern Ireland, western Scotland, Orkney and Shetlands.

KEY FEATURES Thin green-blue crust with prominent circular pore sieves having raised edges.

SIMILAR TO The green-blue colour combined with pore sieves are only found in this species in shallow water in Britain and Ireland. However, further north and in deeper water there are other blue *Hymedesmia* species. *Terpios gelatinosa* is also blue but does not have pore sieves.

Hymedesmia paupertas. Loch Sunart, Highland.

Phorbas fictitius (Bowerbank, 1866)

Phorbas fictitius. Eddystone, Devon.

This thickly encrusting sponge varies from pale orange to deep red. The colour seems to reflect the prevailing water clarity and illumination, with the brightest specimens being on the least turbid sites. The sponge can reach up to 14mm thick and patches may be up to 30cm across. Its surface is covered with circular depressions which contain inhalant pore sieves.

Found in exposed or tide-swept areas on bedrock. Most common in the infralittoral (down to ~20m), particularly on gully walls.

Widely distributed on western coasts of Britain and Ireland.

KEY FEATURES Orange to red encrusting sponge with numerous pore sieves.

SIMILAR TO *Hemimycale columella* has white rims to its pore sieves which contrast with the body colour.

Hymedesmia jecusculum (Bowerbank, 1866) (not described here) is a similar colour and form, but occurs as a much thinner sheet. If in doubt microscopic examination will be required to confirm identification.

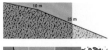

Phorbas plumosus (Montagu, 1814)

A large subtidal specimen of *Phorbas plumosus*. Kimmeridge, Dorset.

A small specimen of *Phorbas plumosus* exhibiting the prominent oscules and feather-like branching channels. Sark, Channel Islands.

Peach to pale orange thickly encrusting (0.5–1cm) sponge forming small cushions (often around 6cm in diameter but large specimens can be over 30cm in diameter). Surface covered with many small bumps with slightly darker branching, feather-like, channels between them giving it its characteristic appearance. Large irregular oscules scattered over the surface. The sponge has a strong smell like iodine or garlic on breath.

Found on the shore under boulders and overhangs, in the kelp zone, and in the shallow sublittoral, usually at sites exposed to waves or current.

Present on all coasts of Britain and Ireland, but most records from Irish Sea coasts of Wales and Northern Ireland and the English Channel.

The name comes from the Latin 'pluma' meaning feather.

KEY FEATURES Peach or pale orange thickly encrusting sponge with channels and bumps on its surface.

SIMILAR TO On the shore the species can be readily identified from colour and surface texture. However, subtidal species can have a less typical appearance with large veins, and here microscopic examination is often needed to confirm the species.

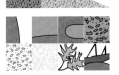

This specimen of *Crella rosea* is mainly encrusting in form but lobes are starting to develop at its bottom edge. Isles of Scilly, Cornwall.

Crella rosea, a lobed specimen. Isles of Scilly, Cornwall.

Pale orange or peach sponge which can be smoothly thickly encrusting or with low rounded lobes. Can form large patches over 30cm in diameter. The surface is usually covered with numerous, round, transparent, bubble-like, pore sieves and there are also large oscules; however, when the sponge contracts, the surface can look smooth and the sponge appears more angular.

Found on bedrock from 2–108m, usually in areas of moderate or strong tidal movement.

Mainly a southern species with most British and Irish records from the south coast and the Channel Islands.

KEY FEATURES Pale orange or peach thickly encrusting sponge with numerous pore sieves.

SIMILAR TO *Desmacidon fruticosum* is yellow to pinky/peach in colour and has taller finger-like projections, but while these often also have grooves down their sides they lack pore sieves.

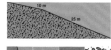

Cliona celata Boring Sponge

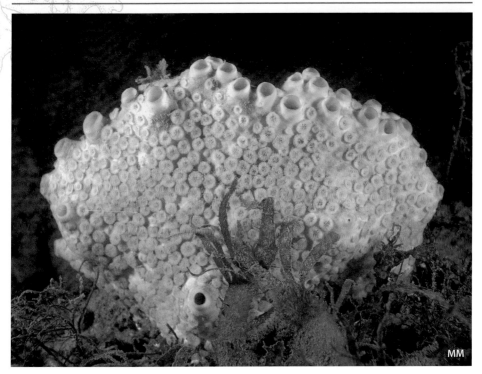

The oscules of the massive form of *Cliona celata* are often situated on the highest parts of the sponge. Lyme Bay, Devon/Dorset.

The massive form of this sponge is a bright lemon yellow, sometimes almost fluorescent yellow, lump or lobe with numerous large flattened circular papillae on its surface. Individual sponges can be very large – over 100cm in diameter.

The boring form is less obvious as the main body of the sponge is hidden inside the substrate of shells or limestone rock, and only the pale yellow circular papillae are visible.

The massive form is found on bedrock. The boring form is often found on dead shells.

The massive form is very common around the western coasts of Britain and Ireland, but not present in the North Sea. The boring form is widespread and associated particularly with oyster and mussel beds.

This species was formerly regarded as widespread in the Atlantic Ocean. However, recent molecular work has shown that *Cliona celata* consists of at least four morphologically cryptic species in the north-east Atlantic and Mediterranean, and that some of these have both boring and massive forms. Two of these species occur in Britain and Ireland; as the type specimen of *C. celata* was a boring individual described from the Firth of Forth one of these represent true *C. celata*.

The scientific name comes from the Latin 'celatus' meaning hidden.

KEY FEATURES Yellow sponge which can either form massive lobes with raised papillae or live cryptically with only the papillae visible.

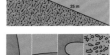

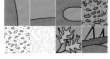

ToG

SIMILAR TO The massive form is unlikely to be confused with any species found in our shallow waters. However, some species (none of which are described here) could be confused with the boring phase: *Pione vastifica* (Hancock, 1849) has smaller red-orange papillae; *Cliona lobata* Hancock, 1849 has pale yellow papillae but they are much smaller and more numerous. *C. caledoniae* van Soest & Berlinger 2009, recently described from cold water coral reefs, has similar papillae but is probably restricted to deeper water. Microscopic examination of the spicules would easily confirm identification as these species all have microscleres.

Some massive specimens of *Cliona celata* can attain over 100cm in diameter. The Skerries, Co. Antrim.

BP

The boring form of *Cliona celata* is often found on dead shells.

Massive or encrusting – with projections

Amphilectus fucorum Shredded Carrot Sponge (Esper, 1794)

The mound form of *Amphilectus fucorum*. Outer Hebrides.

The tasselled form of *Amphilectus fucorum*. Menai Strait, Anglesey.

A pale orange to vibrant orange sponge which has a wide variety of growth forms. Its surface is covered with numerous small pores and there are often large scattered oscules, often along the tops of ridges or mounds. It is thickly encrusting, but often develops projecting tassels, or other structures such as rounded lobes or volcano-like mounds. It has a strong iodine-like smell.

Found in a wide variety of sites from tidal rapids to sheltered sea lochs from the lower shore into the circalittoral. It can be the dominant sponge in tide-swept areas. Grows on rock, seaweeds, hydroids and even sea squirts.

Common on all coasts of Britain and Ireland.

Its scientific name references the fact it is often found amongst fucoid seaweeds.

KEY FEATURES Polymorphic, carrot orange, sponge.

SIMILAR TO The colour and surface texture are fairly distinctive when combined with one of the characteristic tasselled or mounded growth forms. However, simple encrusting forms may need microscopic examination to distinguish from other orange thickly encrusting species.

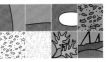

Hymeniacidon perlevis (Montagu, 1818)

A peach-orange to blood-red sponge. Very variable in form. Common on the shore as thin, normally bright orange, sheets on boulders and bedrock – often found in crevices and beneath overhangs. A thicker pinky-orange cushion form is often found on the lower shore on rock and kelp holdfasts. On sheltered lower shores and the shallow sublittoral, thick cushions are found which often have numerous well developed thin lobes and ridges or slightly flattened, irregular, volcano like projections. In silty areas, most of the sponge may be buried and only the tips of these will be visible.

Found on all coasts of Britain and Ireland, although only scattered records from North Sea coasts.

KEY FEATURES Peach to blood red encrusting or cushion forming sponge.

SIMILAR TO The massive form is unlikely to be confused with anything else, but the encrusting form may be confused with other encrusting species (*Microciona* etc.) and may need microscopic examination to confirm identification. *H. panicea* cannot tolerate the very silty conditions in which this species is often found.

A pale pinky-orange sublittoral specimen of *Hymeniacidon perlevis* with numerous projections. Isle of Wight.

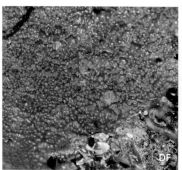

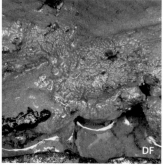

Thin bright orange sheets of intertidal specimens. Penzance, Cornwall and Plymouth, Devon.

Haliclona fistulosa (Bowerbank, 1866)

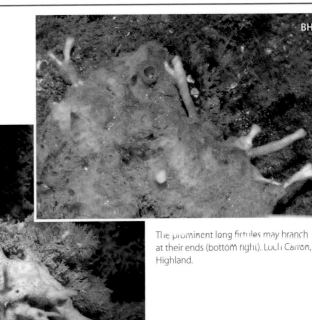

The prominent long fistules may branch at their ends (bottom right). Loch Carron, Highland.

Haliclona fistulosa. Sark, Channel Islands.

Very pale pink, pale peach or white sponge in the form of a crust or low mound. Most specimens bear rounded translucent projections (fistules) and/or long (several cm) solid string-like projections which are sometimes branched at their ends. Some of the translucent projections may be topped with oscules.

Found from the infralittoral to 50m on boulders, bedrock and kelp holdfasts. Usually at sites with some water movement.

A south-western species in Britain and Ireland; records on the west coast up to Shetland but more common from the south-west of England and the Isles of Scilly.

KEY FEATURES White to peach or pink encrusting sponge with long fistule projections.
SIMILAR TO Specimens without fistules could be confused with many pale encrusting sponges (particularly the white/pink form of *Haliclona rosea* (Bowerbank, 1866) (not described here)) and would need microscopic examination to confirm identification.

Haliclona fistulosa, a specimen of which has yet to develop fistules. Sark, Channel Islands.

Desmacidon fruticosum (Montagu, 1818)

A yellow to pink/peach sponge which can be thickly encrusting, but is most noticeable in its characteristic massive form which consists usually of several long finger-like projections joined together at the base. The fingers often have a groove down one side. The sponge can be very large – over 30cm high. If removed from the water, it exudes large amounts of slime.

A deeper water species with most records from 25m or deeper.

Found on southern coasts of Britain and Ireland. It is not a well-known species and further records would be very useful.

KEY FEATURES Large yellow to pink/peach sponge with several finger-like projections, fused at the base.

SIMILAR TO *Crella rosea* has a similar distribution and is a similar colour. However, although *C. rosea* can have lobose projections, it never has very long finger-like ones and its surface has many transparent circular pore sieves.

This specimen of *Desmacidon fruticosum* has developed small nodules on its surface but the characteristic transparent grooves are also clearly visible. The Manacles, Cornwall.

Desmacidon fruticosum, typical finger form, note the channels down the edge of the fingers. Isles of Scilly, Cornwall.

Massive with papillae

Polymastia boletiformis Yellow Hedgehog Sponge (Lamarck, 1815)

Polymastia boletiformis. Purbeck, Dorset.

Bright yellow or pale orange low mound covered with tapering papillae which bear an oscule on their ends. The overall appearance is like a yellow or orange hedgehog. Sometimes the papillae retract, leaving low bumps over the surface of the sponge. The sponge usually has a clean, silt free surface – despite inhabiting silty areas.

Found on horizontal bedrock and boulders, particularly in silty areas.

Common on all coasts of Britain and Ireland.

KEY FEATURES A cushion-shaped yellow or orange sponge with tapering papillae.

SIMILAR TO *Polymastia penicillus* and *Ciocalypta penicillus* also have papillae. However, both of these species have a silt covered basal cushion.

Polymastia boletiformis. The Skerries, Co. Antrim.

Polymastia penicillus Chimney Sponge (Montagu, 1818)

Polymastia penicillus. Purbeck, Dorset.

A pale yellow to orange low cushion or thick crust which bears numerous tapering pale yellow papillae (projections) on its surface. The larger exhalant papillae end in an oscule, and are clearly different to the thinner inhalant papillae. The cushion is usually covered in silt so only the papillae are visible.

Found on horizontal bedrock, particularly in silty areas.

Common on western and southern coasts of Britain and Ireland. Previously known as *Polymastia mamillaris* in Britain and Ireland but that species is currently thought to be restricted to Scandinavia.

KEY FEATURES Low silt covered cushion with pale yellow papillae.

SIMILAR TO There are several other species of *Polymastia* which occur in Britain and Ireland; many are poorly known and several are currently undescribed. Further work is needed to link spicule differences with external appearance. *Ciocalypta penicillus* has conical papillae with a distinct central core.

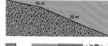

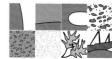

In this specimen the size difference between inhalant and exhalant papillae is very pronounced. The Skerries, Co. Antrim.

Ciocalypta penicillus Cored Chimney Sponge   Bowerbank, 1862

The sponge base is buried in silt or sand, so all that is visible are numerous white or pale yellow conical papillae, normally about 5–9cm high and 0.5cm wide. The papillae are slightly transparent and a central core is visible in the centre of each one.

Appears to be restricted to areas where upward facing bedrock or boulders are overlain by clean sand or gravel, typically in areas with moderately strong wave or tidal action.

Has a south-western distribution in Britain and Ireland with many records from the Channel coast around to north Wales. Scattered records from western Scotland and all coasts of Ireland.

Its scientific name comes from the Latin 'penicillus' for painter's brush, which the fistules are supposed to resemble when dried.

KEY FEATURES Low sediment covered cushion with conical papillae, each with an obvious central core.

SIMILAR TO *Polymastia penicillus* is superficially similar but its papillae are cylindrical rather than conical and lack a spicule core.

Ciocalyptus penicillus, displaying the prominent central core in the papillae. Swanage, Dorset.

Ciocalypta penicillus.
Lyme Bay, Devon/Dorset.

GLOSSARY

Ampulla (pl. **ampullae**) (sea squirt) A flask-shaped swelling on the body of the larva.

Anterior (sea squirt) Nearer to the oral siphon (the 'top').

Aquiferous system (sponge) The network of pores, canals and chambers perforating the body, whereby food and oxygen are obtained from the water.

Archaeocytes (sponge) Cells fulfilling a similar function to stem cells in humans, able to develop into any type of cell ('ancient cells').

Asconoid (sponge) Having a simple tubular aquiferous system.

Atrial cavity (sea squirt) The chamber surrounding the branchial sac.

Atrial siphon (sea squirt) The exhalant opening in the body.

Atrium (sea squirt) The space surrounding the branchial sac. Connected to the exterior via the atrial siphon.

Basal Related to the base.

Benthic Attached to the seabed.

Biofouling The unwanted or detrimental accumulation of organisms on a substrate.

Biogenic Produced by living organisms.

Branching Dividing regularly or irregularly to form a three-dimensional structure.

Branchial sac (sea squirt) The filter-feeding pharynx.

Broadcast A reproductive process in which material is ejected into the water column.

Brood A reproductive process in which offspring are gestated and matured within the body of the parent.

Budding Method of asexual reproduction in which new individuals develop as outgrowths of the parent organism.

Calcareous Composed of calcium carbonate.

Cartilaginous Formed of cartilage, hence quite tough.

Cellulose A complex sugar, constituent of cell walls.

Choanocytes (sponge) Flagella-bearing cells lining the incurrent canals that form the aquiferous system.

Chordate Animals in the phylum Chordata, possessing a nerve cord.

Cilia (sea squirt) Motile hair-like outgrowths from the cells, capable of whip-like beating movement. These are used to create a flow of water and also move the mucous net.

Circalittoral Deeper part of the sea with insufficient light for photosynthesising algae, dominated by animals.

Cloacal opening (sea squirt) The shared opening through which water, faecal matter and gametes from multiple zooids exits a compound sea squirt.

Colonial (sea squirts) Forming a group of closely associated individuals, with organic connections between the zooids. Colonial species are further categorised into stoloniferous and compound forms.

Commensal Living in close association with mutual benefits.

Compound (sea squirts) Colonial species where individual zooids are embedded in a common test.

Conule Cone-shaped projections from the surface.

Conular/conulose Possessing conules.

Cryptic The ability to avoid observation or detection (for predation or anti-predation purposes); may involve camouflage, mimicry etc. Of species, one or more species appearing morphologically similar.

Dichotomous Branching into two roughly equal parts.

Digitate Finger-shaped.

Direct development Reproductive process without a free-living larva in the life-cycle.

Dorsal The upper side of a plant or animal (cf. ventral).

Dorsal lamina (sea squirt) A fold in the wall of the branchial sac, opposite the endostyle, guiding food-enriched mucus posteriorly into the oesophagus.

Encrusting Growing laterally over the substrate to which the organism is attached.

Endostyle (sea squirt) A longitudinal groove in the branchial sac, involved in mucus secretion. Mucus is moved up over the branchial wall by ciliary action and strains food particles from the water before it passes through the stigmata.

Exhalant Relating to the outward flow of water (cf. incurrent/inhalant).

Fistules (sponge) Tube-like projections arising from the sponge surface.

Flagella (pl. **flagellae**) (sponge) Whip-like structure that can move in a synchronised fashion to move water into the body.

Gelatinous Jelly-like in consistency.

Gemmules (sponge) Spore-like 'buds' of reproductive material within a tough protective outer covering, able to remain dormant if necessary under unsuitable conditions.

Globose (sponge) A massive form almost hemispherical in shape.

Globular (sponge) Ball-shaped; may be a regular sphere or irregular oval. Usually attached by a stalk at the base.

Gonad Organ in which reproductive cells are produced.

Gut Tube running from the branchial sac to the anus in which food is ingested and digested. Consists of oesophagus, stomach and intestines.

Hermaphrodite Possessing both male and female reproductive organs.

Hispid (sponge) Having long, closely-packed 'hairs' (often spongin fibres projecting through the surface).

Incurrent (sponge) Inward flow of water (cf. exhalant).

Indirect development Reproductive process with a free-living larva in the life-cycle.

Inhalant (sea squirt) Inward flow of water (cf. exhalant).

Infralittoral Below the lowest tide level, shallow and plant-dominated.

Intertidal Between the highest and lowest levels of tide, on the shore.

Languet (sea squirt) A tongue-shaped projection around the atrial siphon of a zooid.

Lateral Relating to the side(s).

Leuconoid (sponge) A more complicated aquiferous system than asconoid, with more folding and structure to the incurrent canals.

Lobe/lobose (sponge) Rounded lumpish projection on the surface; possessing lobes.

Lobules/lobulose (sea squirt) Small lobes; possessing lobules.

Longitudinal Along the body lengthways, rather than across (cf. transverse).

Mantle (sea squirt) The soft external body wall lining the test.

Massive (sponge) Thick (>10mm) crust projecting significantly from the substrate to which the organism is attached.

Mesohyl (sponge) The layer between the pinacocytes and choanocytes.

Microphagous (sea squirt) Feeding on minute particles.

Microsclere (sponge) A very small spicule, varied in shape.

Morphology Relating to overall shape/form.

Motile Capable of motion.

Notochord A rod-like cartilaginous structure supporting the body in all embryonic and some adult chordate animals.

Oral siphon (sea squirt) The inhalant opening in the body.

Oral tentacles (sea squirt) Structures arranged on a ring muscle around the base of the oral siphon. They prevent large particles from entering the branchial sac.

Oscules (sponge) Larger holes on the surface through which water is expelled.

Oscular chimney (sponge) An upstanding rounded or cylindrical structure on the surface, bearing the exhalant oscule at the terminal end.

Ostia (sponge) Small pores on the surface of a sponge, through which water enters the body.

Ovary Reproductive organ in which female gametes (eggs) are produced.

Oviduct (sea squirt) A tube that carries eggs from the ovary to the atrial cavity.

Oviparous A type of reproduction in which the fertilized eggs are brooded internally until larvae hatch.

Papillae Small round or cone-shaped lumps (sea squirt); hollow strap-like tubes generally >5mm long (sponge).

Papillate Possessing papillae.

Peristalsis Involuntary muscular contraction and relaxation causing wave-like movement.

Pharynx (sea squirt) Anterior region of the alimentary canal.

Pinacocyte (sponge) A contractile flattened cell forming the outer layer of the sponge body.

Plastic Having a variable shape or growth form as determined by environmental conditions.

Pore sieve (sponge) A circular structure on the surface, containing both inhalant and exhalant ostia.

Punctate Dotted with pin-point impressions, punctured (as of the surface of a sponge).

Regress Return to a former state; in sea squirts, to absorb zooids into the colony.

Reticulation Netted (e.g. referring to the visible pattern of channels in the body of a sponge).

Sessile Incapable of motion, fixed to the substrate.

Silica Silicon dioxide, 'glass'.

Siphon (sea squirt) A cylindrical extension through which water enters (oral siphon) or leaves (atrial siphon) the body.

Sperm duct A tube which directs sperm from the testis to the atrial cavity.

Spicule (sea squirt) Calcium carbonate particles that strengthen the test and provide colour, especially in didemnids.

Spicule (sponge) Small structural element of the skeleton, the nature, size and variety of which are often crucial to identification of the species.

Spiculose Possessing spicules.

Spongin (sponge) The collagen-like protein fibres forming the main skeletal structure.

Stellate Star-shaped.

Stigmata (sea squirt) Perforations in the wall of the branchial sac through which water passes into the atrial cavity. Stigmata are arranged in regular transverse rows and their form varies from straight, square to spirals.

Stoloniferous (sea squirt) Colonial species where individual zooids are connected by a basal test and stolon.

Stolons Root-like extensions branching from the base of the body.

Striation (sponge) Longitudinal lines or grooves (hence striated).

Sublittoral Below the lowest tide level, so always submerged.

Subtidal See sublittoral.

Substrate Surface to which the animal is attached. May be hard (rock, boulder, shell, wreckage etc.) or another animal or plant.

Syconoid (sponge) A more complicated aquiferous system than asconoid, with more folding and structure to the incurrent canals, some of which contain flagellae to assist with the flow of water.

Symbiotic A close physical association between two organisms of different species, generally having a mutually beneficial relationship.

Terminal Located at the end/top of a structure (as with terminal oscule).

Test (sea squirt) The cellulose-containing outer layer, also known as the tunic, which overlays the mantle.

Thorax (sea squirt) Part of body containing the branchial sac.

Transverse Lying across the body, perpendicular to the body length. (cf. lateral or longitudinal).

Tubular (sponge) Composed of tubes, or having an overall tube-shape.

Tunic (sea squirt) See test.

Unitary (sea squirt) Singular, not connected to another (zooid).

Ventral The underside of a plant or animal (cf. dorsal).

Viviparous Producing live young rather than laying eggs.

Zooid (sea squirt) Individual organism in a colony.

REFERENCES AND WEBSITES

SEA SQUIRTS

Alder, J. & Hancock, A. (1905). *The British Tunicata*. Ray Society.

Berrill, N. J. (1950). *The Tunicata*. Ray Society.

Brunetti, R. & Mastrototaro, F. (2017). *Ascidiacea of the European Waters*. Edagricole-New Business Media.

Connor, D. W. (1989). *Synoicum incrustatum* (Sars, 1851), an ascidian new to the British Isles. *Irish Naturalists' Journal* 23: 59–63.

Delsuc, F., Brinkmann, H., Chourrout, D. & Philippe, H. (2006). Tunicates and not cephalochordates are the closest living relatives of vertebrates. *Nature* 439: 965–8.

Millar, R. H. (1970). *British Ascidians*. The Linnean Society of London.

Monniot, C. (1969). Les Molgulidae des mers européens. *Mem. Mus. nat. Hist. nat. Paris.* 60(A): 171–272.

Monniot, C., Monniot, F. & Laboute, P. (1991). *Coral Reef Ascidians of New Caledonia*. Editions de L'ORSTOM.

van Name, W. G. (1945). *The North and South American Ascidians*. Bulletin of the American Museum of Natural History, v84.

Picton, B. E. (1985). *Ascidians of the British Isles; a Colour Guide*. Marine Conservation Society.

da Rocha, R. M., Zanata, T. B. & Moreno, T. R. (2012). Keys for the identification of families and genera of Atlantic shallow water ascidians. *Biota Neotropica*. 12(1): 269–303.

SPONGES

Ackers, R. G., Moss, D. & Picton, B. E. (1992). *Sponges of the British Isles – a colour guide and working document*. Marine Conservation Society.

Boury-Esnault, N. & Rützler, K. (1997). *Thesaurus of Sponge Morphology*. Smithsonian Institution Press. repository.si.edu/handle/10088/5449

Chelvadonné, P., Pérez, T., Crouzet, J-M, Bay-Nouailhat, W., Bay-Nouailhat, A., Fourt, M., Almón, B., Pérez, J., Aguilar, R. & Vacelet, J. (2014). Unexpected records of 'deep-sea' carnivorous sponges *Asbestopluma hypogea* in the shallow NE Atlantic shed light on new conservation issues. *Marine Ecology* 36: 475–484.

Goodwin, C. & Picton, B. E. (2011). *Sponge Biodiversity of the United Kingdom. A Report from the Sponge Biodiversity of the United Kingdom Project May 2008–May 2011*. www.dassh.ac.uk/dataDelivery/filestore/1/1/8/9/8_16efc02c99add1d/11898_def0ddd5afdbd09.pdf

Hooper, J. N. A. & Van Soest R. W. M. (Eds.). (2002). *Systema Porifera: a guide to the classification of Sponges. 2 volumes*. Springer-Verlag.

Picton, B. E. & Goodwin, C. E. (2007). Sponge biodiversity of Rathlin Island, Northern Ireland. *Journal of the Marine Biological Association of the UK*, 87(6), 1141–1458. doi.org/10.1017/S0025315407058122 and www.divernet.com/marine-life/p298636-the-joy-of-sponge.html

Picton, B. E., Morrow, C. C. & Van Soest, R. W. B. (2007). *Sponges of Britain and Ireland*. www.habitas.org.uk/marinelife/sponge_guide/index.html

Van Soest, R. W. M., Boury-Esnault, N., Hooper, J. N. A., Rützler, K., de Voogd, N.J., Alvarez, B., Hajdu, E., Pisera, A. B., Manconi, R., Schönberg, C., Klautau, M., Picton, B., Kelly, M., Vacelet, J., Dohrmann, M., Díaz, M.-C., Cárdenas, P., Carballo, J. L., Ríos, P. & Downey, R. (2018) *World Porifera database*. www.marinespecies.org/porifera

Van Soest, R. W. M., Boury-Esnault, N., Vacelet, J., Dohrmann, M., Erpenbeck, D., De Voogd, N. J., Santodomingo, N., Vanhoorne, B., Kelly, M., John, N. A. & Hooper, J. N. A. (2012), Global Diversity of Sponges (Porifera). *PLoS ONE* 7(4): e35105. doi.org/10.1371/journal.pone.0035105

GENERAL WEB RESOURCES

Habitas - Encyclopedia of Marine Life of Britain and Ireland
www.habitas.org.uk/marinelife Based in the Ulster Museum and maintained by Bernard Picton and Christine Morrow, this photographic guide covers a selection of the larger animals which live around the coasts of Britain and Ireland. it is intended for divers and marine biologists who need to be able to recognise species *in situ* and is illustrated by underwater pictures. It is a good source of updated information on species.

MarLIN – The Marine Life Information Network
www.marlin.ac.uk Based at the Marine Biological Association in Plymouth, the site provides much information about species, with photographs for most, and habitats. It also contains information about biodiversity and conservation for key species.

Marine Species Identification Portal
www.species-identification.org This website provides open access to scientific information on thousands of different marine species worldwide from plankton to marine mammals, including identification keys It is a portal to over 30 specific projects

Encyclopedia of Life
eol.org/pages/1486/overview This website aims to provide descriptions and pictures of all species on earth.

The Dutch Ascidians
www.ascidians.com This website includes a selection of worldwide species with a range of photographs.

DORIS – Données d'Observations pour la Reconnaissance et l'Identification de la faune et la flore Subaquatiques
doris.ffessm.fr/find/species A French marine biology site with numerous sea squirts and sponges included.

European Marine Life / Mer et Littoral
www.european-marine-life.org or www.mer-littoral.org A French resource with an English version available. The authors (Wilfried and Anne Bay-Nouailhat) are active members of the Facebook NE Atlantic Tunicata and Seasearch Identifications Groups.

National Biodiversity Network
nbnatlas.org The main resource for distribution and mapping of British and Irish species, this site allows you to view distribution maps and download data by using a variety of interactive tools. This is the public repository for all Seasearch information and has the benefit that you can search for marine data from a number of sources in a single location.

Seasearch Identifications, NE Atlantic Tunicata and NE Atlantic Porifera
www.facebook.com/groups/seasearch.identifications
www.facebook.com/groups/248476708561508 (NE Atlantic Tunicata)
www.facebook.com/groups/238934849520932 (NE Atlantic Porifera)
Facebook groups for those interested in identifying unusual species, with discussions and identification help from active diver-recorders.

Seasearch
www.seasearch.org.uk
The site for all the information about Seasearch and how to get involved. You can download recording forms and guidance and find out what courses and diving surveys are planned. The site also gives access to over 300 reports from diving surveys around Britain and Ireland.

MD

A Seasearch diver recording a rocky reef in the Farne Islands, Northumberland.

Seasearch diving and recording

This guide has been produced mainly to help Seasearch divers and snorkellers to identify the sea squirts and sponges they see on their dives. We hope it will also lead to more records of species which divers have not previously been able to recognise.

Seasearch is a volunteer underwater survey project for recreational divers throughout Britain and Ireland to record observations of marine habitats and the life they support. The information gathered is used to increase our knowledge of the marine environment and contribute towards its conservation.

Seasearch data has helped to define the boundaries of areas for conservation, recorded the presence of rare and unusual species and provided information for local groups to campaign for protection of their local marine life and habitats. The data are held both by local record centres and centrally and are available for anyone to consult on the internet through the National Biodiversity Network (NBN). Go to **www.nbn.org.uk** to see it.

Divers can participate in Seasearch training courses at different levels suitable to their knowledge and experience. The Observer Course provides an introduction to marine habitat and species identification and survey methods. The Surveyor Course is for more experienced recorders and there are also Specialist Courses which provide participants with more information on specific groups of marine life or additional survey techniques.

In addition to a national coordinator for the project, there is also a network of local coordinators in many coastal areas who organise Seasearch survey dives and training. We can also provide training and talks in other areas on demand. For further information see the Seasearch web site at

www.seasearch.org.uk

Seasearch is a partnership between the Marine Conservation Society (MCS), The Wildlife Trusts, statutory nature conservation bodies and others, co-ordinated nationally by MCS and co-ordinated and delivered locally in England by Wildlife Trust and MCS local co-ordinators.

Seasearch hopes that this guide will encourage even more divers to complete Seasearch forms after any of their sea dives. You can download Seasearch forms from our website or obtain them from any of the coordinators.

Any dive can be a Seasearch dive!

PhL

Index

Entries in **bold** refer to the main species accounts

Adreus fascicularis 132

Amphilectus fucorum 127, 175, **185**

Aplidium cf. *glabrum* **55**

Aplidium densum **67**

Aplidium 'honeycomb' **67**

Aplidium nordmanni 18, **56**

Aplidium ocellatum **57**

Aplidium pallidum **58**

Aplidium punctum 16, **59**, 63

Aplidium 'strawberry' **61**

Aplysilla rosea 125, **163**

Aplysilla sulfurea **162**

Archidistoma aggregatum **54**

Ascidia conchilega **69**

Ascidia mentula 17, **70**, 85

Ascidia virginea **72**, 114

Ascidiella aspersa 20, **73**

Ascidiella scabra **74**

Asterocarpa humilis **93**

Axinella damicornis **138**

Axinella dissimilis 125, **130**

Axinella flustra **143**

Axinella infundibuliformis 125, 127, **140**

Black Tar Sponge **158**

Boltenia echinata **85**

Bolteniopsis prenanti **86**

Boring Sponge **183**

Botrylloides diegensis **94**, 97

Botrylloides leachii **94**, 95

Botrylloides leachii var. *radiata* 95

Botrylloides spp. **94**, 115

Botrylloides violaceus **94**, 96

Botrylloides sp. X 102

Botryllus schlosseri **99**

Breadcrumb Sponge **174**

Cactus Sea Squirt **85**

Carpet Sea Squirt **41**

Chimney Sponge **190**

Chocolate Finger Sponge **137**

Ciocalypta penicillus **191**

Ciona intestinalis 16, 20, **76**

Clathria barleei **142**

Clathrina coriacea 105, **149**

Clathrina lacunosa **150**

Clavelina lepadiformis 17, 18, 19, 22, **29**, 65, 113, 115

Cliona celata **183**

Compass Sea Squirt **93**

Compressed Purse Sponge **148**

Cored Chimney Sponge **191**

Corella eumyota **77**

Corella parallelogramma 21, **78**

Crater Sponge 127, **178**

Creeping Sea Squirt **79**

Crella rosea **182**

Crumpled Duster Sponge **138**

Dendrodoa grossularia 22, **104**, 149

Dercitus bucklandi **158**

Desmacidon fruticosum **188**

Diazona violacea 23, **34**, 115

Didemnum coriaceum **36**

Didemnum maculosum **38**

Didemnum maculosum var. *dentata* **39**

Didemnum pseudofulgens **40**

Didemnum vexillum **41**

Diplosoma listerianum **44**

Diplosoma sp. 1 **47**

Diplosoma spongiforme 10, 19, **45**

Distaplia rosea **53**

Distomus variolosus 38, **106**

Distomus hupferi 106

Dysidea fragilis 127, **161**

Elephant Hide Sponge 125, 127, **171**

Endectyon delaubenfelsi **139**

Eugyra arenosa **81**

Fluted Sea Squirt **73**

Football Sea Squirt **34**

Gas Mantle Sea Squirt **78**

Golf Ball Sponge 125, **151**
Goosebump Sponge 127, **161**
Grantia compressa **148**
Halichondria bowerbanki **175**
Halichondria panicea **174**
Haliclona cinerea **165**
Haliclona fistulosa 127, **187**
Haliclona oculata **131**
Haliclona simulans 125
Haliclona urceolus 125, **145**
Haliclona viscosa 127, **164**
Halisarca dujardinii **155**
Hemimycale columella 127, **178**
Hiatella rugosa 11
Homaxinella subdola **135**
Hymedesmia paupertas **179**
Hymedesmia sp. 11
Hymeniacidon perlevis **186**
Iophon hyndmani **177**
Iophon nigricans **176**
Leathery Sea Squirt **111**
Leuconia nivea **159**
Leucosolenia spp. 125, **147**
Lightbulb Sea Squirt **29**
Lissoclinum perforatum **48**
Lissoclinum weigelei **49**
Lycopodina hypogea 121
Mashed Potato Sponge **172**
Mermaid's Glove Sponge **131**
Microcosmus sp. **87**
Microcosmus claudicans 87, 89, **92**
Molgula citrina 81
Molgula complanata **84**
Molgula manhattensis 81
Molgula occulta 81
Molgula oculata 81
Molgula socialis 81
Molgulids **81**
Morchellium argus **62**
Mycale lingua **173**
Myxilla incrustans 127, **169**

Myxilla rosacea **170**
Ophlitaspongia papilla **157**
Orange Cloak Sea Squirt **96**
Orange-tipped Sea Squirt **77**
Oscarella sp. 117, **156**
Pachymatisma johnstonia 125, 127, **171**
Perophora japonica **79**
Perophora listeri **80**
Phakellia ventilabrum 125, **141**
Phallusia mammillata **75**
Phorbas fictitius 11, **180**
Phorbas plumosus **181**
pinhead sea squirts 30
Polycarpa pomus **109**
Polycarpa fibrosa **107**
Polycarpa pomaria **108**
Polycarpa scuba 32, 107, **109**
Polyclinum aurantium 64, **67**
Polymastia boletiformis 125, 127, **189**
Polymastia penicillus **190**
Polysyncraton bilobatum **50**
Polysyncraton lacazei **51**
Prawn Cracker Sponge 125, 127, **140**
Purse Sponge 125, 127, **146**
Pycnoclavella aurilucens 13, 30, **31**, 38
Pycnoclavella producta 30, **32**
Pycnoclavella spp. **30**
Pycnoclavella stolonialis 30, **33**
Pyura sp. **87**
Pyura microcosmus 87, **88**
Pyura squamulosa 87, **90**
Pyura tessellata 87, **91**
Quasillina brevis **153**
Raspailia hispida 125, **133**
Raspailia ramosa **137**
Salp 14
Sand-encrusted polyclinids 67
San Diego Sea Squirt **97**
Sea Orange 127, **166**
Shredded Carrot Sponge 127, 175, **185**
Aplidium elegans **65**

Aplidium turbinatum **66**
Spiky Lace Sponge 125, **147**
Spongionella pulchella 119, **144**
Stelligera montagui **136**
Stelligera stuposa **134**
Star Sea Squirt **99**
Stolonica socialis 17, **110**, 113
Styela coriacea 105
Styela clava **111**
Suberites carnosus 125, 127, **152**
Suberites ficus 127, **166**
Suberites massa **167**
Sycon ciliatum 125, 127, **146**

Synoicum incrustatum **67**
Terpios gelatinosus **154**
Tethya citrina 120, 125, **151**
Tethyspira spinosa **160**
Thymosia guernei **172**
Trididemnum cereum **52**
Ulosa digitata **168**
Volcano Sponge 127, **164**
White Lace Sponge **149**
Yellow Hedgehog Sponge 125, 127, **189**
Yellow-ringed Sea Squirt 16, **76**
Yellow Staghorn Sponge 125, **130**